HOW TO GET A

HIGHLY PAID JOB IN THE CITY

HOW TO GET A

HIGHLY PAID JOB

IN THE CITY

RICHARD ROBERTS
and
LUKE JOHNSON

**KOGAN
PAGE**

Copyright © Richard Roberts and Luke Johnson 1987

All rights reserved

First published in Great Britain in 1987
by Kogan Page Ltd, 120 Pentonville Road,
London N1 9JN

British Library Cataloguing in Publication Data

Roberts, Richard
    How to get a highly paid job in the City.
    1. Financial institutions — Vocational
    guidance — England — London
    I. Title   II. Johnson, Luke
    332.1'023'4212   HG186.G7

    ISBN 1-85091-474-5

Printed and bound in Great Britain by
Richard Clays, Bungay, Suffolk

Contents

Part 2: Targeting the Job

Introduction

Big bang means big bucks for those lucky enough to work in the City. With the recent boom in financial services, the advent of the global market—in which London plays a key role—and deregulation, the City is rapidly becoming one of the most exciting places to work in.

What's more, the recent liberalisation has led to the rapid demise of the old boy network which in the past dominated some of the more traditional areas of the finance industry. Foreign companies with financial muscle are more concerned with your ability to produce than the colour of your tie or the tone of your voice. Add to this the large number of new jobs now being created and you can see why the best talent is rapidly being sucked into the business.

Whether you want to work in finance for a high salary, prestige, or simply the buzz from working at the financial heart of the UK, this book should give you some idea of what to expect. It aims to give some insight into how the city actually works and the different types of jobs which are available. Obviously, it isn't possible to give a detailed breakdown of the entire multitude of careers, so we have tried to concentrate on the more interesting or more common ones. Equally, it isn't possible really to know whether you will thrive in a particular job until you have tried the work yourself.

Money

The vexed question of renumeration is bound to be raised when talking about jobs in the City. The Americans now pay very high starting salaries—some graduates can pull up to £25,000 pa and that's for starters!—and the Brits have been forced to follow suit. In fact, some of the large British stockbroking firms are now offering equally ridiculous compensation. One recent example

was a firm offering £20,000 pa for a person to do a bit of filing an
to write one newsletter a month!

So how should you approach it? The standard method is to g
for the highest bidder. Be very careful if you take this route. Firs
think about the various packages on offer. There is not a grea
deal of difference after tax between £20,000 and £15,000 pa. I
you find a firm which is offering £15,000 which you think you wi
enjoy working for and where you think you can thrive, take it i
preference to a firm which offers you more money but where yo
don't like the atmosphere. If you are right and you thrive at th
£15,000 job it won't be long, maybe six months or a year, befor
they up the ante. Into the bargain you won't mind getting up a
7am in the morning to go to work. But if you take the £20,000 p
job and you don't like it, the chances are that it won't be lon
before you and your firm part company. Remember that i
employers are paying that amount of money they usually expec
results—fast. If they don't get them they'll sling you straigh
back on to the streets.

Living in London

Although in this book we do cover careers which are no
necessarily based in the City, notably accountancy and to som
extent fund management, most of them are London based and
offer little or no prospect of getting out of London. For mos
people this doesn't present a problem and is one of the benefits o
having a job in finance. You will find that the City has a friendly
villagy type atmosphere where people generally get on well with
each other and know a number of the people in their own line o
work. In short, it is very civilised. However, you will occasionally
come cross interviewers who are worried about employing people
who have never lived in London before. This concern is something to be prepared for.

Part I: The Job Profiles

1. Eurobond Sales

Long hours and hard sell, all for the sake of a red Porsche and a house in Kensington

As one of the most stressful occupations in the City, Eurobond sales is a perfect example of the dual emotions of fear and greed in operation. Fear that you might burn out or lose your job before you earn enough money to retire; greed inspired by the vast fortunes to be earned. This line of business has reached almost mythical proportions and is often cited as the number one Porsche-driving yuppie profession. Talk of six-figure salaries and burnout by the age of 30 only helps to enhance its reputation.

So what is a Eurobond and how can it make you a fortune? Eurobonds are relative newcomers to the world of finance. Originally they were used by multinational companies looking for new ways of financing overseas expansion. Since then they have developed and are now used not only by companies world-wide but also by governments which want to borrow money. Essentially if an organisation wants a loan it can use a Eurobond issue. It issues bonds which it will pay interest on until they expire or, in the case of perpetual notes, for ever. So if Megacorp wants to borrow $45 million it could issue bonds up to this value. It will then pay an agreed rate of interest on these bonds until they are due for redemption. This simply means in the case of, say, a 10-year bond that in 10 years' time the holder will receive the face value of the bond back from the company. So in this respect they are a form of short-term borrowing.

However, as time has gone by more adventurous forms of lending have been devised: for example, the perpetual floating rate note. This has two features which differ from the normal Eurobond. The first is that the bond does not have a redemption date. In other words, you will receive interest on the bond but you will never get the capital back. Second, the interest rate is not a fixed percentage but is floating. In other words, the company might pick a yardstick interest rate-for example, the London inter-bank offered rate (LIBOR)-and fix the interest rate at, say, 0.25 per cent above whatever that rate might actually be. So if LIBOR is, 10 per cent on 1 March the company will pay an interest rate of 10.25 on the face value of the bond on that particular day, but if the rate alters to 9.8 per cent the following day the company will pay only 10.05 per cent.

Eurobonds are big business. In 1986 almost $187 billion was raised in the Eurobond market compared with just $24 billion in 1980. The institutions which make the running in this field are the large international banks such Citicorp, Morgan and Chase Manhattan, not to mention the huge Japanese banks such as Daiwa and Nomura. They are responsible for organising the financing deals for customers who, as mentioned previously, might be major companies, governments or international organisations. In the first instance the bank will ascertain the needs of the client and then try to arrange the best sort of product. So apart from the traditional Eurobond you will hear of FRNs, swaps and Eurobond convertibles. For this service the bank obviously takes its cut.

Once the deal has been struck the bank then has to arrange underwriting. Obviously, the company or organisation which is trying to raise the money would not be at all happy if it didn't get the full amount because the bank could not sell enough of the bonds. To get round this problem the bank agrees to underwrite the issue. In other words it will buy all the bonds on offer, thus guaranteeing that the company gets its money. Naturally the bank will take a fee for this which might involve, for example, selling the bonds for more than it bought them for. But it also has to be appreciated that the bank is taking on a big risk. It can get around this to some extent by arranging sub-underwriting. Under this arrangement it approaches other banks and asks them to take on part of the risk by agreeing to buy some of the bonds and then selling them through their network of salesmen. Nevertheless the 'lead' bank as it is called is unlikely to be able to arrange sub-underwriting for the whole issue, so it will rely on its salesmen to sell the bonds as quickly as possible when they have been issued.

This is where the infamous Eurobond sales person comes into play. Apart from the slightly bizarre and specialised nature of the products there is no real mystery to what the sales person is doing. Like any other sales person they simply have to shift the products at the best possible price. However, you are selling to highly sophisticated institutions and for this reason the market has gained a reputation as being strictly for the professionals; and as such anything goes. Unlike most other financial markets there is a distinct lack of regulation in the Euromarkets. So when things start to go wrong there are no umpires or regulatory bodies to fall back on: you simply have to fight it out among yourselves.

A typical recent example is the market for perpetual floating rate notes. When someone has bought an instrument such as a Eurobond they do so in the belief that they will be able to sell it on to other buyers just as you can buy and sell shares. A new Eurobond issue is very similar to the flotation of a company on the Stock Exchange. There is the initial issue where people subscribe for (in the case of shares) or are sold (in the case of Eurobonds) financial assets. These are only pieces of paper but they can represent large sums of money, and if the issue is to be successful it is important for people to think that they will actually be able to sell the shares or bonds as and when they wish.

The buying and selling of bonds-or indeed shares-which have already been issued takes place on what is known as the 'secondary' market, because the market is essentially dealing with second-hand goods. In Eurobonds this market generated business of $3.1 trillion in 1986. Large banks and financial institutions will make markets in certain kinds of Eurobonds, which means that they will be prepared to buy and sell them as and when people wish. They will usually make a profit by charging a spread: they will have different buying and selling prices (exactly the same as the system banks operate when you want to buy or sell foreign exchange). However, whereas on the stock market, market makers are obliged both to buy and sell the shares in fair weather or foul, the Eurobond market is largely unregulated (to some extent this is one of its major attractions). So in 1986 when the market for perpetual Floating Rate Notes (FRNs) fell flat because the Japanese institutions decided they weren't worth buying any more, there were a lot of people who wanted to get rid of them. Unfortunately, the market makers in Eurobonds are not forced to take them on board so a lot of people ended up with burnt fingers, either because they couldn't find anyone to sell the bonds to, or if they could, they could only get about 75 per cent of what they had paid for them.

So that's a brief rundown on how the market works. What about the job? Naturally, if you're dealing with large institutional investors such as pension funds or insurance companies who have hundreds of millions or even billions to invest it's important to know a lot about the market. When you're selling them a bond you have to convince then that it's the right thing for them to buy at that particular time. To be able to do that you need to know a lot about the client and his investment requirements. This is not necessarily particularly complicated but it is vital, as you want to avoid continually pestering him with irrelevant products which don't meet his requirements.

The products you sell will be determined by the bonds which your bank hold. At any one time the bank's traders will hold quantities of bonds either because your bank is sponsoring an issue or because they have taken a 'position' as part of their market-making function. Either way it is the salespersons' job to sell those bonds. The salespersons should identify those clients who might be interested in the bonds, phone them up and try and sell the bonds. It's important to remember that it's a professionals' market. It is very difficult to sell a client a duff product or, as the professionals say, to 'stuff' a client, because he is likely to be as knowledgeable as you.

This is where the secret weapon of the bond salesperson comes into play. They all work on high octane fuel and because of this are capable of getting into the office at, wait for it, 7.30 am every morning. Before they get into work they will be expected to have read the *Wall Street Journal* and/or the *Financial Times*. When they get into the office they must immediately start to gauge the mood of the market by looking at their Reuters news screens to see what happened in Tokyo overnight. By 8 am it will be time for morning prayers. Here the bond dealers tell the salespeople what products they have to sell and the quantity, and the salespeople will then be left to get on with the job.

Just like any other sales job there is no secret about where you get your clients from. The bank doesn't usually provide you with a useful list of clients when you arrive. No way. Remember that this is selling at its dirtiest and each one of those clients could be a potential gold mine so other salespeople would have swallowed them up long ago. Instead, you have to go out and find your own customers. Thanks to the international nature of the job it's useful to be able to speak a foreign language or two. If you can, then your potential client base will be wider, although it must be said that at the end of the day English is the international language of finance, so foreign languages are not absolutely essential.

Remuneration

The big earnings potential comes into the equation simply because you are dealing with major clients who spend large amounts of money. When an institution is buying Eurobonds it won't be dealing in thousands but in millions or tens of millions and that goes for every time you make a sale! So if your commission is only a fraction of a percentage you will still be looking at very big money. Typically, you'll start on about £15,000 per year for this type of job although the Americans will tend to pay better. But when you get your feet under the table the sky's the limit. A reasonably successful salesperson can expect to be earning about £50,000 (including bonus) within two years, although guaranteed salaries as high as £150,000 are not all that unusual!

If designer clothes and red Porsches are your scene then perhaps you ought to look at the world of the Eurobond salesperson. Walking around a typical trading floor you'll see enough gold jewellery to make Mr T jealous. Hardly surprising when you consider the sort of salaries which are earned by these people. Nevertheless, there is the down side to consider. Burnout at an early stage is often mentioned as a significant disadvantage. Most of the banks deny that this happens but try telling that to someone who can actually feel the ravages of time hitting him-at just 28! It's just as important to get the right company. The whole business is now starting to look quite mature and some people in the market are predicting major shake-outs over the next few years.

Finally, you should take a close look at your personality. Not only is this side of the business about selling but *hard* selling. This sort of environment is not conducive to the fairly relaxed office atmosphere of other less strenuous occupations. And when you consider that by getting into work at 7.30 am and leaving at 6 pm you will spend most of your conscious life in such an environment, it is very important to ask yourself if it's really worth it!

The list of major firms starts on page 85.

2. Stockbroking

Sales

Soft sell leads to big money for the institutional sales specialists

Most British stockbroking firms deal for their bread-and-butter business in UK shares on behalf of institutional investors. The key players in this process are equity salesmen, who liaise directly with fund managers. Traditionally, most City broking houses were run by the senior sales partners, who generated vast commission income for the firm, and earned enormous salaries for themselves. Since big bang in October 1986, however, commission rates for big institutional trades have fallen by up to 50 percent and the old relaxed style of broking, when commission rolled in whatever happened, has rapidly disappeared. A new feature in the securities industry is the advent of market makers, replacing the old dual capacity system with jobbers, operating on the Stock Exchange floor. Instead, major banks and corporations act both as agents and principals, by simultaneously conducting trade on behalf of investors and running a book in various shares themselves.

These dramatic changes have brought major upsets and opportunities to stockbroking and for sales staff. Crucially, salesmen and women must work with market makers in their firm to compensate for the lower commission levels achieved by making a turn on shares held by the firm itself. In this new world, it is likely that the most able and professional salespeople will be better rewarded than ever before: Warburg Securities, one of the largest post-big bang conglomerates, recently announced widespread bonuses averaging £120,000 each for all its senior equity traders, owing to a successful first year. However, those lazy individuals who coasted before on good old boy contacts and ignore research will find their salary package distinctly less than their old partner drawings.

Assuming there is no dramatic market collapse, the opportunities to enter stockbroking via sales are excellent. Big banking outfits-UK, European, US and Japanese-now recruit on the university milk-round, with a general bias towards Oxbridge graduates. They take on students with a keen interest in business and the stock market, preferably an understanding of commerce and economics, and extrovert personalities. They look out for the classic characteristics which make up good salesmen and women: an outgoing and friendly manner, but a positive and businesslike approach to work, and the ability to close a sale.

At this stage it should be pointed out that institutional sales staff do not operate in high-pressure boiler rooms, with morning warm-ups, shouting supervisors, phone directory cold-calling and frequent obscene rebuffs. They talk all day by phone to selected, qualified clients at a sophisticated level, and while their aim is to solicit commission-generating orders, it is not in their interest to 'stuff' clients into the first share they can think of. Successful salesmen work by developing long-term relationships with money manager clients through offering sound advice and regular contact. Although fund managers are besieged by calls from brokers all day, they need the market information which brokers provide, and will act on good ideas or attractive lines of stock.

Most young trainee sales staff will work as assistants to more senior sales members in an open-plan trading room. Their day will begin between 7.30 and 8 am, when they will listen to the 'morning meeting' address by several analysts from the research department (see page 00), which should generate some good buying ideas to put to clients. They will also report to clients the opening market conditions as suggested by their market makers, with perhaps a view on the influence the previous day's Wall Street closing price and Tokyo's trading will have on the initial price trends. They will have to have read and digested the morning financial press (ie the FT, and possibly *The Times*, *Daily Telegraph*, or the *Independent*), and might offer comment on the reporting coverage given to the previous day's news.

During the day sales staff will initiate calls to clients and receive buying and selling orders unsolicited. They will work with analysts both face-to-face and by reading and interpreting the written research laid before them. They will constantly be keeping clients in touch with annual figures announced or acquisitions, bids or takeovers made. Important economic or political news with market implications will also be monitored. Sales staff normally work on a busy, quite noisy, open-plan floor filled with green monitors and hundreds of phones. They will be constantly checking prices and receiving news via the various electronic screen services provided by the Stock Exchange and commercial vendors such as Reuters.

While most client contact is by phone, sales men and women often organise meetings, presentations, and lunches where they get to know their customers. The classic venue is the brokers' lunch, when a broker will host an event at which a company MD or chairman will discuss the business of a quoted concern with perhaps half a dozen fund managers around a table. These occasions serve to demonstrate close connections between the broker and the public company, and allow salesmen to get to know their clients at a personal level. They also permit everyone to have a damn good feed! Sales staff will also on occasion work with analysts on developing an understanding of a particular company and visit that company, perhaps taking various major institutional shareholders.

Increasingly, specialist salesmen are appearing. These staff are not generalists who cover the entire UK market, and really only regurgitate the analysts' opinions of shares. Instead they concentrate, like analysts, on one sector, but spend most of their time talking to institutional clients rather than writing and talking to companies. They work very closely with their opposite numbers in the research departments, and will tend to liaise with buy-side (institutional) analysts rather than pure fund managers. Since they are still relatively rare, respected specialist sales people can command substantial salaries.

The salesmen and women will become closely involved in most corporate operations the firm conducts, such as new issues, or takeovers conducted on behalf of quoted client companies. Senior staff might well participate in highly confidential and senior discussions regarding any marketing matters relating to flotations or bids and deals. Thus, an institutional salesman would be expected to contribute to a debate about the pricing of a new issue, a highly sensitive topic which balances the demands of the vendor shareholders with the expectations of the market. A salesman can therefore enjoy a significant role in such matters without having to become concerned with more tedious accompanying matters such as new issue Long Form reports and approvals from the Stock Exchange Quotations Department. If a salesman has to flog the shares, he will surely know best just what the clients will swallow.

The Stock Market of 1987 is wide open to women. Although certain male chauvinists still wield power, this is rapidly diminishing, and increasing numbers of women are populating the trading floors of the City.

Remuneration

Overall, salesmen and women tend to receive a higher proportion of their pay by way of bonus than staff in the research and corporate finance departments. Depending on the firm, the commission they generate from their roster of, say, 15 major pension funds, insurance companies, and unit trust managers, will be reflected more or less overtly in the bonus they receive. Normally up to 40 per cent of total pay is received in this way. Trainees can expect to start on about £12,000, which might rapidly accelerate to around £30,000 for an able middle-ranking sales figure, to £75,000 and beyond for top performing sales people. It is normal for most firms to offer staff, after a probationary period, a company car, the value of which will relate to basic pay. Other benefits might include a cheap mortgage (an interest rate of perhaps 5 per cent below the commercial rate is common), private medical insurance, and a non-contributory pension scheme. An important perk which is normally offered by stockbroking firms to all staff is a reduced rate of commission on stock market dealings, and most stockbrokers have usefully supplemented their incomes by pa (personal account) trading. However, since the advent of Ivan Boesky and insider dealing scandals, most firms have forbidden account dealings: and all employees of a member firm of the Stock Exchange have to deal through that firm, in order that their dealings may be monitored.

Market Makers

Barrow boys make a killing playing with billions

Market makers are a new breed within the stockbroking fraternity, supplying the function jobbers used to provide, but within bigger securities groups. Essentially, market makers offer two-way prices in shares and deal with sellers and buyers as principal. They turn a profit on the spread between the bid

19

(buying) and offered (selling) prices. They execute orders directly with other market makers and with their own sales arm on behalf of clients.

Most market-making arms have been established by the old core of jobbing executives; for instance, Barclays de Zoete Wedd's market-making arm is based on the old Wedd Durlacher jobber, while the Smith New Court broking outfit (backed by N M Rothschild) is focused on the jobbing skills of Smith Brothers.

Market makers come from disparate backgrounds. A trading mentality rather than an intellectual approach is demanded. Trainee market makers are recruited from the age of 18 upwards, and the rewards for successful individuals are enormous: several senior market makers receive compensation of over £250,000 per year—a glance through Smith New Court's annual report reveals just how well paid they are! But at the same time, the price for failure is rapid dismissal. The sudden closure of Midland Bank/Greenwell Montagu's market-making capacity just six months after big bang came as a shock to many in the stockbroking community. But the move was accompanied by statistics showing how expensive bad market-making can be: losses of over £5 million during the period. So the position is not for someone who rates job security as his highest priority– perhaps being a traffic warden would be more suitable!

Market makers work in teams and need to be glued to their electronic dealing desks all day, from 7 am till 6 pm, with a sandwich at their desks for lunch. They are constantly buying and selling lines of shares and adjusting the indicated and firm prices at which they may have to deal respectively. For each transaction they undertake, they must attempt to keep a relatively balanced book—and make a profit on their holdings. The capital required to run books of shares is colossal, so the dealing returns need to be impressive to justify the ongoing investment. Market makers each run a book for a specific number of companies within an industrial sector. In this way, the market maker can acquire a knowledge of the sector, familiarise him or her self with the companies that comprise that sector, and begin to understand some of the influences on their share prices. It is not normally expected that a market maker will have direct experience of working in the industrial sector for which he is to make markets.

The powers of concentration needed to become a competent market maker are considerable. The ability to give snap price quotes, and do rapid mental arithmetic for 10 or more hours a day requires stamina and dedication, but there is enormous satisfaction to be derived from running a major book successfully—and mouth-watering bonuses! The technical requirements of the job are not massive, although any applicant should have a strong interest in and a reasonable understanding of the stock market.

Market makers have to pass the Stock Exchange's Registered Traders Examination, which tests basic knowledge of the practices and procedures of markets. An ability to assess market trends, which is largely developed through experience rather than theory, separate good from mediocre market makers. Market makers are frequently not graduates, but come from backgrounds in similar trading environments, such as foreign exchange, money broking, commodity dealing or bond dealing. People with sales experience are looked upon favourably, particularly those from horse-trading type work like computer-broking. Seemingly very few market makers are women, although this situation will change.

Apart from the senior managers, most market makers are under 30. They are either worn out at this age, or bored, and (if they've been successful) rich enough to retire—at least for a few years. Younger traders are thought to have quicker reactions and greater mental capacity for rapid calculations. These factors mean there should be plenty of opportunities in market-making over the next year or so. But having said that, where 25 houses make a market in a particular stock, many will be losing money because of over-competition. While certain agency-only houses, such as James Capel, are achieving considerable success without a market-making arm, others may be forced into a position to offer large lines of stock, ie make limited markets. Overall, market-making represents one of the most exciting, highly paid, but exhausting and risky career openings in stockbroking, and should only be attempted by energetic, tough extroverts.

Private Client Work

Quite often the training ground for stockbrokers

One of the most common areas for graduate trainees to commence in a City stockbrokers is the private client department. This section accepts buying and selling instructions

21

from private individuals rather than institutions, and manages portfolios on behalf of individuals.

With the number of private shareholders rising to 9 million in the last few years, thanks to the huge growth in share ownership encouraged by share option schemes and government privatisation issues, private client broking has boomed. Those bigger broking houses specialising in private client work, such as Quilter Goodison, Wood Mackenzie, and Kleinwort Grieveson, have taken on considerable numbers of staff to cope with demand. Consequently, the employment opportunities in this area have blossomed. This followed a long period when most brokers were heavily concentrating on expanding their institutional sales side, as the pension funds and insurance companies rapidly accrued more of the pool of available shares.

Beginners will start an apprenticeship in this department because they can learn the ropes without normally risking enormous sums of money or offending extremely powerful clients. Usually, a trainee, post A levels or straight from university or polytechnic, would work with a more senior staff member. A trainee might initially handle administration only, while watching how the tutor treats clients, offers advice, and executes orders. A good level of patience is required for private client work, since many of the people you speak to will not be stock market sophisticates, or will have a lot of bad ideas which need destroying – gently! Clients will tend to be either discretionary or non-discretionary. This means that the broker determines their investment requirements, and then manages a share and gilt portfolio for them, or alternatively the client will simply use the broker as an agency to execute buy or sell orders. Some clients need a service in between these two extremes, where a client might normally make his own investment decisions, but occasionally takes a tip or advice from the broker, and needs fairly regular updating on the market and specific prices.

A big broker will receive regular guidance from its economics and equity research departments as to investment policy and current share recommendations. Private client staff will then interpret this information and devise suitable strategy for the 100 or so clients they look after on a discretionary basis. These portfolios might vary in size from £60,000 to £6 million. Discretionary clients will be sent regular written updates from their broker examining the performance of the portfolio and describing new purchases and recent sales. Private client brokers must call market makers direct to deal or will work through an in-house dealer, who might make client purchases in bulk.

Much of the time will be spent on the phone, either advising clients or executing orders. The build-up of private client business in the last couple of years has meant that staff are kept very busy, although much of the new business is rather small, dealing only in the big issues like BT, British Gas, and TSB. However, with a new Tory administration and the prospect of further privatisations, the growth in individual share ownership can only continue, and with it, demand for broking private client service. Many private clients start dealing through their banks, but soon graduate to brokers once their requirements become frequent.

Private client staff will start the day around 8.45 am with a morning meeting, relaying market trends and specific news and recommendations. Much of the day will be spent on relatively mundane matters, such as checking settlement or dividend payments, and reshuffling portfolios. Private client staff tend to work later in the evening, often until 7 pm, since this is the time when their clients are actually reachable, and reports can be given.

The work is suitable for those who enjoy talking with and learning about a wide variety of active and passive investors from all walks of life. There's plenty of excitement from small punters who like to speculate on penny shares, and there are often substantial private clients who have great personal fortunes. Clients tend to give their broker considerable respect; unless they work with a boiler house outfit pushing dubious OTC stocks, a private client trainee should not expect to be hard-selling share ramps every day to people who don't want to listen.

Very often private client staff will move into other departments, such as institutional sales or research, or even settlement. But the most common area is into broking fund management. Big brokers such as Hoare Govett manage several billions of pounds of pension and private client money, and have teams of in-house money managers looking after this. They spend their days talking to broking salespeople and analysts and companies, and in some ways perform the job of discretionary private client work on a massive scale. From a broking fund management group, someone can easily move to one of the big unit trust managers such as Henderson Administration, to a big pension fund such as CIN (the Coal Board), or to an insurance company like the Prudential.

Remuneration
Pay as a junior private client staff member will not be spectacular—perhaps £8,000 to begin with, rising to, say, £15,000 within a couple of years. Increasing responsibility can see this salary climb to £50,000 or more for a competent and hard-working individual. Those private client members who can bring in big new clients are the best rewarded, and so selling ability is once more required to get to the top.

Research

A multi-skilled discipline which combines the attributes of an accountant, an economist, a writer, an orator and a salesman, stockbroking researchers are the intelligentsia of the City

A securities analyst investigates quoted companies and prepares written reports on them. He attempts to understand shares so that he can accurately estimate the future prospects of the firms underlying them. The earnings progress of companies will tend to be reflected in their share price. By better advising institutional investor clients as to which companies have the best management, markets and products, a stockbroker will make better returns for his clients and more commission for himself and his firm.

All the big London stockbrokers have a research department of between 20 and 50 analysts. Analysts are drawn from a wide range of backgrounds, since they tend to focus on a broad spread of industry sectors. Major industry classifications include building materials; contracting and construction; engineering; stores, banking and insurance; electricals and electronics; oil and gas; and food manufacturing. Frequently analysts come from an industrial background relevant to the types of companies they will study: thus someone researching metal bashers might have worked in engineering.

Overall, the position of research analyst combines various skills: that of an accountant, an economist, a writer, a speaker, and a salesman. Although an analyst does not need an ACA or ACCA qualification, around 25 per cent of analysts are qualified or part-qualified chartered accountants. An experienced analyst is expected to feel comfortable breaking down an annual report, in order to interpret the financial information presented in it. He should be able to form a view of a company's results and quality of profits, and be able to project earnings into the future. He must have a thorough grasp of the profit and loss account, the balance sheet, and source and application of funds and cashflow statements. The various technical stock market aspects and rules of listing companies, takeovers and mergers, rights issues and the like should all be comprehended. The latter details can certainly be acquired through practice and by attending the various courses which excellent organisations such as Financial Training and BPP run—and which most broking houses pay for.

It is important to stress that would-be analysts should not be scared off by the idea of undertaking incredibly complex paper transactions or calculations. The level of accounting and financial expertise required to prepare sound research and reach appropriate conclusions is not over-burdensome. The best story along these lines is when Alan Sugar (multi-millionaire boss of Amstrad) went to the very proper English merchant bank, Kleinwort Benson. They asked him what he thought his p/e (price/earnings ratio) was. He replied, thinking they meant gym work, 'Oh, about 20 press-ups a day.'

Probably more important than an ability to manipulate figures is a feel for investment and the stock market. This does not mean rote-learning of such grand ideas as the Efficient Market Theory; rather, it means the market nose to really recommend certain shares at certain times, and to make reasonable guesses about what's going up and what's going down. In essence, all stockbrokers do is say to investors, 'Buy X and sell Y'. Giving this advice involves much more than pure fundamental research of a particular company's business environment. Without a fascination for the way the stock market works, and an eye for a bargain share, it is difficult to become a successful analyst.

Once an analyst has reached a conclusion on a company and its shares, he has to translate his thoughts into words, both written and spoken. While analysts do not have to possess great literary merits, they must be able to prepare coherent, intelligible written documents. These might include both a qualitative discussion of a company's activities, markets, competitors, history and prospects, and a quantitative review of its trading performance and finances. Analysts should be able to write fairly punchy copy quite quickly, rather like journalists. Increasingly, they will key material directly into a word processor, for rapid transmutation into a printed work, which will be immediately distributed to an audience of perhaps 750, mostly outside the firm. A typical output expected would be one longer document (say 20 sides) per month, and eight shorter pieces of just two sides.

Equally important is the analyst's verbal discussion of his investment views. Every morning at around 8am, brokers stage a 'morning meeting'. This is a brief presentation over a microphone to the collected institutional salesmen and women by a few analysts of one or two specific investment ideas for that day. Throughout the day analysts will also discuss with individual salesmen recent company visits or breaking news on an acquisition or a set of interim results. An analyst is expected to call institutions like pension funds and insurance companies—BP Pension Fund and the Prudential Corporation, for example—as well as specialist investment managers like M & G and Gartmore. These outfits manage billions of pounds invested in shares and gilts, and require constant updating on their various portfolio holdings if they are to maximise investment returns for their beneficiaries. Analysts must offer honest, pertinent opinions, preferably directed towards initiating a buying or selling order from the client—which will earn brokerage commission for the firm.

Since fund managers are paid to listen to analysts, the selling element of the job hardly compares to cold-call telesales of magazine space, say, rather, analysts are involved in a news-disseminating role which has a persuasive bias. Hence, someone who loathes the conventional concept of door-to-door hard selling should not feel put off by this aspect of security analysis. But a the same time, prowess at convincing clients to follow your views is an invaluable asset for any analyst.

A significant, and perhaps underrated, element of an analyst's job is meeting with senior management in industrial companies, and reporting back any worthwhile findings. Normally analysts liaise with the most senior personnel in a quoted company—normally the finance director, treasurer, and managing director or executive chairman. Analysts are exceptionally privileged in their easy access to such powerful business figures—because, it must be said, these directors value stockbroker circulars which encourage people to buy their shares and buoy up the share price. Analysts must be able to relate to such people and prove they are an educated audience, with a good knowledge of the given industry and company. In interviews and at preliminary results meetings and brokers' lunches, analysts must be able to put intelligent but worthwhile questions–even if they are not overtly friendly questions. However, analysts must get on well with company management, since a company is under no obligation to give friendly audiences to analysts. One of the reasons why 'sell' printed circulars for circulation outside a firm are so rare in the UK is that a company is likely to close its doors to that firm and its analyst from that point on.

Around a quarter of an analyst's time is spent visiting companies, either alone or with a group of rival analysts. This aspect of the job is immensely attractive, since it means one is not anchored to a City desk all day, and gets guided tours of premises and installations by the most qualified people of all–often the very founder of the business! Indeed, it's occasionally difficult not to let the high level of communication with companies as an analyst go to one's head. It is important to remember that they are not just talking to you–they are addressing a powerful spread of big money managers via your written circulars, phone calls, and sales force.

Normally, companies will work with analysts to ensure that any published brief is factually correct, even if the management don't agree with the analyst's subjective conclusions. Analysts will also organise visits to companies by groups of fund manager clients, and business lunches held within the broker's dining rooms. On these occasions, one or two top people from a company will explain their business and accept questions in a more relaxed setting than a formal presentation with audio-visual paraphernalia.

With increasing internationalisation of securities markets, and London a global centre of finance, the opportunities for foreign travel for analysts are excellent. European, Far East and American institutional investors are becoming ever more influential, and may require occasional servicing through a visit to their home city. In addition, many industries encompass concerns with worldwide interests, such as BAT Industries, Hanson Trust and Grand Metropolitan. Analysts are from time to time invited to visit the foreign subsidiaries of such UK giants. And if an analyst specialises in foreign equities, such as Australian stocks, he would be expected to visit that country at least twice a year to meet the management on the ground. And finally, the growth of multinationals in many commercial fields means that analysts in specific sectors can no longer ignore a company even if it is not a UK-based business—an example is News International, Rupert Murdoch's business in the publishing sector.

Analysts typically work in teams of two, or occasionally three, but will normally cover companies separately rather than be joint authors of everything. Many broking houses have traditionally seen research as a slightly less important function, but the big bang has strengthened the position of analysts. Institutional investors now demand first-class research ideas and attention if they are to channel business through a broker and award commission. Consequently, all the key players in London have beefed up their research capacity, and now offer coverage of virtually all major industrial categories.

Analysts must also co-operate with the market makers within a firm, if the broker possesses that capacity. The market maker in an analyst's stocks should be kept informed of crucial short-term news which might affect his book. Frequently, an analyst will have to act on an announcement and without knowing all the facts, react decisively to the investment implications of the news.

A further department where an analysts' input is valued is the corporate finance division. These staff members supervise quoted companies who are clients. They advise the company on all matters relating to the stock market, from an initial flotation, to acquisitions and mergers, takeovers, rights issues, and the like. An important member of the team which might pitch to become broker to a company will normally be the industry specialist from the research department. Not only might he provide useful market and competitor insight, he will prepare the definitive research papers on the company on any sets of results or big deals. Often the corporate finance department will have several special analysts attached full-time. They would tend to be qualified accountants, since the work is of necessity more concerned with analysing and advising companies on transactions, rather than offering recommendations to investing clients.

Analysts are partially observers, in that they report on a company and its business without becoming involved. But they also create serious written documents, which can often have a profound effect on the price of shares. One reads any day of the week in the financial pages' 'market notebook' section of how a company's price went up because of a bullish circular by one of the big brokers. Analysts are more than ever being quoted in the press, and even appearing on radio and TV. While the average analyst's salary might not be as high as an accomplished institutional salesman or foreign exchange dealer, an analyst benefits from developing a reputation and expertise in an industry completely outside the stock market. Thus analysts probably have an alternative career available within their specialist sector, while most highly paid dealers and brokers within the City are vulnerable to a heavy market downturn. Having said that, pessimists have been predicting an end to the present bull market for some years, and no sharp decline can yet be discerned, so perhaps this cushion is irrelevant. Analysts can quite quickly become established names, within their firms and with important clients, on various shares: a number of analysts below 30 are currently considered the experts in a specific field. However, the potential for job development can be limiting. Essentially, analysts might increase in market stature and reputation, but the work they do will not necessarily alter. Unless they become head of the research department, the amount of managerial responsibility available to most analysts is minimal. More often than not, the better, more ambitious analysts graduate either to specialist or general salesmen (the pay and managerial prospects are better) or to the corporate finance department.

But overall, there is no better job for a young, intelligent graduate with an enquiring mind who wants to make a career in the stock market and establish a reputation quickly. Research departments in stockbroking firms do take on applicants direct from university, perhaps as assistants or affiliated to the economics department. Degrees in mathematics, economics or business studies are an obvious disadvantage, but are by no means a prerequisite. But the most fertile breeding grounds are the major accountancy practices, business journalism, and statistical firms such as Datastream, Extel and ICC.

Remuneration
The respect in which analysts are held within many firms has grown, and salaries have risen commensurately. A reasonably competent graduate with perhaps two years' experience in the relevant industry, or two years' accountancy training, can expect to start on around £15,000 a year, with a possible bonus. If they

How to Get a Highly Paid Job in the City

prove competent, analysts can easily be earning £30,000 including bonuses, and benefits such as a company car and a low-cost mortgage, within two or three years—by the time they are 26! Very senior analysts can command substantial salary packages ranging up to £150,000. A determining factor in the market value of an analyst is the rating the analyst achieves in the annual survey of fund managers, organised by Extel and published every summer. Coming in the top three within a sector is worth a lot to the firm in terms of increased business and ensures a high remuneration. Datastream also conduct an important treasurer's survey of analysts, published every autumn.

The list of major firms starts on page 89.

3. Commodities

As financial services enjoy an unprecedented worldwide boom, financial futures provide the growth in the commodities business

The commodities business covers a whole range of activities which can be conveniently divided into three categories: agricultural products such as cocoa, sugar and coffee (commonly referred to as *softs*), metals such as gold, silver and aluminium (*hards*), and financials such as currencies and government bonds. In fact the term 'commodity' is perhaps a little misleading and it is probably more accurate to describe the business as the futures industry.

Futures exist in order to allow people to hedge against risk. They developed because of the long time span between a commodity actually being harvested and its delivery to market. In this time span the price could alter dramatically, thus exposing the producer to the risk of not receiving enough money from his harvest to cover his costs. One way of avoiding this potential problem is to sell your crop in advance so that you will know exactly how much money you will receive for it when it reaches the market-place. By doing this you can ensure that not only will your costs be met but also that you make a profit. Equally, the end user of the commodity will be able to guarantee the price which he will pay for the product. This is useful as commodities are in many instances raw materials which are major costs in a production process.

In this sort of scenario there is risk on both sides of the equation. The producer runs the risk that when his product finally reaches the market-place it will have increased in value so he won't obtain as high a price as he could have done. On the other hand, the user runs the risk that the price of the commodity will fall by the time of delivery. If the fall is particularly dramatic then he might be forced to reduce the price of his end product. An example might be a major oil company which bought oil forward

31

before the price slump in 1986. In that sort of situation it would be forced to reduce the cost of its refined products such as petrol and could well end up making a very big loss.

Commodity brokers exist to try and reduce this risk by offering expertise on the particular markets in which they operate. The broker will be judged by his ability to give the client the best advice thus, hopefully, avoiding any major losses. Of course, in many of the old established markets such as sugar, coffee and tea the producers and to a large extent the users will carry out their own research into the market-place and will in most instances make their own decisions about how to play the markets. However, this is not the case in the financial futures market which is still relatively young. Here there is a great amount of volatility both on a short-term and long-term basis which means that there is an increasing need for brokers with specialised knowledge. This demand means that most opportunities in commodities are now based in the financial futures market.

Financial Futures

There are basically four distinct occupations in the financial futures field: dealers, salesmen, analysts and client liaison. Dealing requires the ability to develop an instinct for how a market works and what actually makes it tick. This means that gut feeling has a large part to play and, for the most part, people educated to degree level or higher do not fit the mould. Thinking and reasoning do not play a large part in the dealer's role: he simply has to see a situation and react to it. When the situation changes he must react to that too without letting the thought process cloud his judgement. This is especially important in a fast moving environment such as commodities where prices can move for or against you in a matter of minutes or even seconds if particularly important news, economic or otherwise, has been released. The dealer needs to develop an instinct to know when a market is about to turn and be able to react when it does. By moving fast enough he should be able to fulfil the classic role of cutting losses and running winners.

Most dealers have worked their way up through the ranks of the brokerage firm, probably starting as junior clerks and progressing as and when their employers saw fit. Indeed, in the early days of financial futures trading in the UK a lot of floor dealers on the London International Financial Futures

Exchange (LIFFE) market were former telex operators who managed to convince their respective employers that they should have a chance at dealing in the market.

Next on the list come salesmen, whose job it is to get clients for the company. The nature of the financial futures market means that salesmen will be dealing with highly sophisticated clients, so in order to ensure the most efficient use of staff, most financial futures brokers differ from the conventional sales-oriented outfit by giving the salesman the specific job of simply opening doors and bringing clients into the company. Once he has done this his function is largely completed and he will go off to find new clients.

A high level of education is not an essential prerequisite for the salesman's job. What is essential is the selling mentality, a good deal of motivation, a lot of psychological knowledge and 'more front than C&A'. Perseverance and the ability to take on responsibility are very important qualities for a salesman, because in most organisations there will not be the facilities to treat them with kid gloves. However, they only require a very low level of pure market knowledge. Their job is simply to open the door and dangle the carrot, but as soon as the client starts to bite they will back off and leave the client liaison people to take over. As with dealers, salesmen will in many instances work their way up through the ranks.

Recognising that it is very difficult both to be a good salesman and to look after clients properly at one and the same time, most financial futures brokers employ client liaison executives to take over where the salesman left off. Client liaison is one of the major growth areas in financial futures and would be one of the areas most suited for graduates. Client liaison or account executives fulfil two functions. Firstly, they have to generate business by gaining the trust of their clients and getting them to act on their recommendations (thus generating commission). In this respect they are very similar to salesmen. At the same time they need to have a detailed knowledge of the market in which they are operating. This helps for two reasons: they will be able to make informed decisions and hopefully recommend the right strategies for their clients, and their sort of clients will usually be financial institutions who have a good knowledge of the markets they are dealing with. In order to be able to get business from these people you have to impress them with your knowledge and prove that your ideas can work for them.

How to Get a Highly Paid Job in the City

Client liaison involves understanding your client's requirements and then applying these to the particular market. As futures trading involves hedging against risk this will usually entail finding out what sort of risk exposure your client has in the nature of his business and then finding ways that he can hedge against them. For example, many large companies such as Jaguar, rely heavily on exports to make a living. This means that they are automatically exposed to the wild fluctuations in the foreign exchange markets. Jaguar, for example, exports a large proportion of its cars to the United States. This means that the company will receive US dollars for the cars which it sells over there. If the US dollar rises against sterling, then for every dollar it earns in the US it will receive more sterling. But if the US dollar weakens against sterling—which has been the case since late 1985—then the company will receive less sterling for every dollar it earns in the US. Here we have a classic example of a company which, through no fault of its own, is exposed to a risk which can have a dramatic effect on profits but about which it can do nothing. One way of trying to reduce the losses is to hedge in the foreign exchange market. Here's how it works.

Assume that a business wins a contract to export to the United States. It will receive $1.5 million for the equipment which it is selling. The current exchange rate is $1.50 to the pound, so on conversion the company will receive £1 million. However, the company won't receive the money for six months and there is always the possibility that the dollar will weaken against sterling in that time. The company knows that if it receives £1 million for its exports then it will make a profit of £100,000. So if the exchange rate falls below $1.666 to the pound the company stands to make a loss. To get around this problem it can lock into the current exchange rate. It can do this by buying the right to sell £1.5 million at a rate of $1.5 to the pound in six months' time. This immediately removes the risk, enabling the company to plan ahead in a sensible manner.

There is a multitude of companies both large and small which have exposure not only to currency risks but also to interest rate risks (if they have high borrowings). In addition, large institutions investing millions of pounds have similar risks, along with risks inherent in their level of investment in the stock market. For all these people financial futures are useful hedging instruments. Perhaps the most exciting aspect of the industry is that there are still many companies and institutions which could benefit from the use of such instruments but still don't use them.

Given that a client liaison executive will spend most of the day talking to clients assessing their exposure and discussing ways of reducing risk, he will need to be both literate and numerate. He has to be able to sell his own personality so that the client will have faith in his judgement and he needs to be able to acquire a good in-depth knowledge of the market-place so that he can spot the opportunities available for his client.

Analysis

The fourth type of opening is available in analysis. For this you really need to have a degree in a relevant subject, such as economics, and the ability to think analytically. An analyst's job is to assess, usually with the aid of a computer, where a particular market will be under different scenarios. For example, an analyst might be faced with the problem of where the gilt market will be if the exchange rate for the dollar falls from $1.50 to $1.40 to the pound. These analyses are usually fairly short term as they are carried out with the specific intention of generating business (ie a client wants to know now what will happen next week, not in three years' time). With such short time-scales the only really sensible approach is to use technical analysis or charts. Here the analyst will simply look at historic price data in graphical form and from this try to discern any patterns which might give a clue as to where a particular market is headed.

Most of the time the analyst will be working to orders from the salesman, who will need information for a prospective client. Eighty per cent of an analyst's time is accordingly devoted to current market situations, ie what will happen today, tomorrow or in a month's time, and only a small proportion of time will be spent on client servicing (ie preparing circulars on long-term trends etc).

Remuneration

While remuneration packages tend to be high for people in the commodities business (basic salaries of £30,000 + bonus + car after only a few years if you are successful) it should be remembered that it is extremely stressful. Usually new employees will be given three to six months to settle into their new workplace and find the areas in which they are most suited, but after that the gloves are off. As with any highly competitive sales/commission orientated job, there is a lot of pressure to produce results and fools are not suffered gladly. Hours are long as well. Brokers need to know their markets because they will be dealing with highly sophisticated clients. As markets become more and more international (especially in financial futures) so global events will affect what happens to the UK market. This means that brokers need to get in early to find out what happened the night before in Tokyo so that they know roughly what to expect when the markets open up in London. Although it is difficult to generalise about hours worked it is not uncommon for people to be in between 7.30 and 8am and work right through till 6 or 7pm with no break for lunch. This sort of workload takes its toll and people who can't cope with it will drop out fairly quickly.

Another point to bear in mind is the different types of employer. Recent comment has focused on the high rates of pay offered by American employers. Hand in hand with this they expect a high degree of loyalty and their approach is extremely hard-nosed. Employees are expected to produce the goods constantly and if they don't they will soon find themselves out on the street. American employers also tend to treat their European staff differently from their own nationals, and if things start to go wrong, no prizes for guessing who's first on the chopping block.

While career prospects are good within the futures industry, especially in financial futures, and the rewards are doubtless there, it has to be said that it is a highly specialised field to work in. Although it is possible to move from job to job within the industry it would be difficult to find another occupation which you could easily fit into. What's more the activity tends to be concentrated around the City of London so unless he moves abroad—possibly to the United States or the Far East—a broker will spend his working life in London.

The list of major firms starts on page 91.

4. Fund Management

The puppet masters who call the tune for brokers and industry

Fund managers are professional money investors. They buy (and sell) equities in the UK and overseas, gilts, bonds, property and various other valuables which appreciate over time. They are now massively important on the British stock market, controlling around 75 per cent of all shares. There are three main types of organisation involved in fund management activities: the pension funds; the insurance companies; and the specialist fund management groups, looking after such things as unit trusts and investment trusts. These groups range from the huge Prudential Assurance to tiny local authority pension fund manager groups.

The prospects, pay, and power of fund managers have all recently improved. Since big bang, fund managers have been able to negotiate commissions with stockbrokers, who buy and sell shares for them; thus the institutions have been more courted than ever. While historically fund managers have been passive investors, they have in recent years become considerably more active, in some cases demanding more energetic moves from the managements of companies in which they invest.

There are at least 150 potential fund management groups in Britain; around a quarter of the opportunities are in Edinburgh, where there is a considerable money management population. Normally big groups will give fund managers specific areas of responsibility, such as Far East investments, or several industrial categories. They also separate out the managers and analysts, who simply advise the managers, but do not make investment decisions. Substantial money management groups even have an in-house dealing department, to execute buying and selling orders for the group.

Fund managers are largely concerned with two activities: managing investments, and gaining new portfolios to manage. This second category only really concerns specialist management groups—the dedicated pension and insurance funds have a captive customer! The groups such as Touche Remnant, M & G, and the merchant bank groups such as Morgan Grenfell and Warburgs, must often pitch to manage funds or advertise for money to look after. Thus the marketing side of the job is crucially important, but is often neglected by prospective fund managers.

Beginners to fund management will help with preparing presentations to new clients by demonstrating the impressive performance of funds under the group's control. Management groups usually charge an annual fee for managing and administering the portfolios they look after—often based on the size of the fund. This cost would cover all the extensive paperwork associated with the buying and selling of shares or bonds and the registration and taxation matters. Junior fund managers straight from polytechnic or university would frequently have a spell in the settlements and administration department before moving on to the actual management of investments.

The core business of fund managers remains the investment of money. Much of this is directed towards fixed income stocks, or in the UK, gilts. There are juicy profits to be made from switching in and out of various gilts, so that the funds manager's job is not simply to buy a gilt, sit on it, and then eventually sell it. In order to produce above-average returns, he must use some of his cash to make quicker profits. Overall, fund managers are now under considerable pressure to achieve short-term out-performance from the monies they manage. Although over time it has proved remarkably difficult to beat the returns achieved by simply investing in a random selection of stocks, fund managers must justify to their clients the fees they extract. Individual fund managers are nowadays partially rewarded on the quarterly performance of their fund, and so they have a great incentive to invest astutely. If the performance of the funds they manage consistently fails to do well, they face possible demotion—or even the sack.

Fund managers will spend virtually all day on the phone. They talk largely to brokers, listening to their interpretation of the market's outlook, and ideas for investments. They closely follow results of the companies they invest in. They are intimately concerned in new issues and takeovers, where often they are required to underwrite the issue of new shares. They need always to bear in mind that they have to report, via trustees, to beneficiaries of the money they manage—indirectly, everyone who invests with a bank, or building society, or in investment or unit trusts, or has a pension. They must believe a share will rise, but quick speculative profits are not normally appropriate—they are investing for continuing returns five, 10 and 20 years hence.

There is growing opportunity for fund managers to meet the people who run the businesses they invest in. Often accompanied by brokers, fund managers may take all-day trips to view the plant of an industrial concern in which they may be substantial shareholders. A classic ceremony in the City is the broker's lunch, where management will be invited to talk to a select group of fund managers. These individuals have enormous power, since they decide where considerable sums of money are invested. Consequently, the directors of public companies are only too pleased to meet with them and convince them of the merits of their particular company as an investment. It's important for fund managers not to be too gullible, since there are plenty of bullshitters in the City, both among company promoters and stockbrokers. In fact, some of the very best fund managers cultivate a healthy cynicism. It is interesting that in *Punch* magazine's annual poll of the Most Hated Fund Manager of the Year, the top scoring managers often also run some of the best performing funds—they just ask harder questions.

Fund managers do not only invest in UK equities. More and more UK institutional money is being invested overseas, as the fashion for specialist foreign unit trusts demonstrates. The opportunities for travel abroad are therefore extensive, although a typical trip might involve as many as five broker or company meetings every day for a week. As ever, the fund manager will need to be able to distinguish between those companies which are above average, and those which will under-perform.

A further area of investment is in real estate, both in the UK and abroad. The percentage of pension and insurance money being put into property in the UK has steadily declined over the last few years, but this trend is likely to change with falling interest rates and better relative yields from property, as shares rise in value. Insurance companies and pension funds increasingly are proactive investors in development schemes, providing not only development finance, but often putting together the team to carry out the development. Normally, every big property tender proposal will have a big institutional partner—and often several. While many funds require property specialists with surveying qualifications and estate agency experience to run these departments, others are less rigid, and will give recruits training. Yet again, the fund managers are powerful figures, deciding in many cases whether to commit several millions of money to a single property project, which will not achieve a return for the investors for some years. The detail required before finally plunging can be arduous, but if the project succeeds, a fine new building rises out of the ground, and pension beneficiaries achieve a good return, the fund manager can justifiably feel proud.

At a more senior level, fund managers are quite often invited to join the boards of public companies in which they are substantial investors. Occasionally, they can play a major role within the company's management—a case in point being Montagu Investment Management's Lord Stevens, chairman and driving force behind the major publishing house, United Newspapers plc. Where a management group, such as Ivory & Sime in Edinburgh, manage a number of investment trusts which are quoted on the Stock Market, then at least one fund manager would sit on the board. Some fund management groups, such as the Merchant Navy Investment Management Group, are corporately active and become involved in takeovers. Usually, however, fund managers are entirely passive investors, only having a major role to play when they accept or decline an offer for their shares during a hostile bid contest.

Many fund management groups are independent, and owned by the managers themselves. Junior staff can expect in time to qualify for share options. Gartmore, Henderson, and Warburg Investment Management are three examples of separately quoted investment groups. There are other private, but independent companies such as Fidelity and Touche Remnant.

Big groups have an in-house administration function, which deals with contracts, records, accounts, transfers and performance measurement. This last matter is of enormous importance to the success of individual fund managers and the entire organisation, since many trustees judge each management group against its rivals purely on the merits of published performance tables. Right at the top of the management tree will be trustees in the case of a pension fund group or a board of directors for specialist money managers. They tend to formulate policy decisions, but not interfere in the day-to-day buying and selling moves. In good fund management groups, relatively young managers can expect to run several millions of pounds at reasonable discretion after a shortish training period–supervised and approved by more senior management.

Remuneration
Girls are treated quite as well as men in job applications. Salaries and promotion will also be totally comparable. Initial pay might be £10,000 for a graduate, moving to £30,000 for a successful executive in the late twenties and early thirties. Senior fund managers can earn £80,000. Recent published figures showed several Mercury Asset Management directors making around £1 million a year! The larger independent fund management groups such as Ivory & Sime, GT Management, and Templeton will offer senior staff share options. There always remains the opportunity at some point to break away and form an independent fund advisory service–the relatively low start-up capital requirements can help make such a suggestion viable.

The list of major firms starts on page 93.

5. Insurance

Lloyd's is still for insiders

Insurance companies represent a massive part of the financial services industry in the UK. Although faced with strong competition from abroad, particularly the United States, the UK insurers have still managed to maintain a very strong position in the world market-place. There are several types of career which are associated with the insurance industry, the best known in the City being Lloyds and investment management (see Chapter 4).

Insurance companies themselves can be conveniently divided into two groups: those which specialise solely in life assurance and those which specialise in all types of insurance (commonly referred to as the composite insurers). Life offices, as the name suggests, make their money by providing people with life assurance. So if a person dies before a certain specified age (for example 60) their estate will receive a lump sum payment from the company. Nowadays it is very common for people who take out life assurance policies to receive a payment whether they die or not. The company itself can make a profit through its ability to assess accurately the likelihood of a person dying during the time span that the insurance policy covers and by so doing adjusting its premiums so that unless something quite drastic happens it will be able to meet its obligations and show a nominal profit. However, he bulk of the profit will come from the successful management of the premiums which the company receives from the people it is insuring. As only a certain percentage of these will have to be paid out over the year the rest can be invested to produce a useful return. Composite insurers, on the other hand, have a more hazardous existence. It is far more difficult to predict the likelihood of claims when the company is covering a diverse range of risks such as fire, motor and aviation. Naturally, under such circumstances the company will rely on its ability to accurately assess the possibility of a certain event happening (for example, a car being stolen in the West Midlands) and will have to adjust its premiums accordingly. Composites are also faced with the problem that large natural disasters such as tornadoes or hurricanes in the US (a large proportion of their business is written there) can drastically affect the equation. Again, as with life companies, the composites rely heavily on their investment management teams to keep the profits rolling in.

In many people's minds Lloyd's is synonymous with insurance. It conjures up images of derring do and risk taking on a grand scale for big rewards. Despite the scandals which have rocked Lloyd's over the past few years it still has a major part to play in the world insurance market especially in the areas of re-insurance and special risks. The two scandals which have most affected Lloyd's concerned brokers Alexander Howden and Minet. In both these cases millions of pounds had mysteriously 'disappeared'. This was damaging not only because the broking firms concerned were large and well respected, but also because the Howden case was not uncovered until an American company took Howden over. Naturally the discovery of losses on such a huge scale attracted a great deal of adverse publicity in the US. Thanks to these scandals and others besides, Lloyd's has undergone a number of changes over the past few years but it remains to be seen how effective these will be in curbing abuses of the system.

Lloyd's itself is essentially organised into syndicates which tend to specialise in ensuring specific sorts of risk, such as shipping. The syndicates consist of a number of 'names'. Some of these will be members of Lloyd's but the vast majority are complete outsiders. They undertake to cover any losses which the syndicate might incur (if it has to pay out on a claim) and in return get a share in any of the profits which it makes. On the plus side, being a name at Lloyds has certain tax advantages; on the negative side the names in a syndicate are liable for all the losses the syndicate incurs. So a name could theoretically lose everything if something went drastically wrong.

There are effectively two opportunities open to graduates at Lloyd's as either underwriters or brokers. If a syndicate is to be a success, ie make money instead of losing it, it needs to have a highly skilled underwriter at the helm. An underwriter has the task of assessing the risks of a piece of business which is offered to him and from there accurately determining the correct premium. If he gets it too high he might not get the business but if he gets it too low then the syndicate could soon run into difficulties. When a broker is looking for underwriters to take on a piece of business such as the insurance of an aeroplane he will not expect one syndicate to take on the whole risk. Instead he will approach a number of underwriters. So another part of the underwriters task is to decide how much of the risk his syndicate should accept. Naturally for the more common types of insurance the large companies will be able to deal with the business as effectively and as cheaply if not cheaper than Lloyd's. It is the more specialised types of insurance risk such as satellite insurance where Lloyd's will score points. In some cases Lloyd's will be the only organisation willing to offer insurance. This is especially so for the more esoteric forms of risk. Indeed, it is the innovative side of Lloyd's which has kept it very much alive despite all the problems which have beset it over the past few years.

Specialised knowledge is not necessarily a prerequisite for being an underwriter at Lloyd's. Some of the risks are so specialised that it would be extremely difficult to quantify the risk involved anyway. In many cases experience will be by far the best way of learning. As an active market-place underwriters at Lloyd's often have to make virtually instantaneous decisions so it is as important to know the people you are dealing with as to know the type of risk you are insuring. The specialised nature of Lloyd's business means that underwriters will tend to concentrate on relatively small areas of business. As their specialism becomes more developed so they will tend to become the experts in particular markets. This combined with the fact that the underwriter's ability to make the right deal at the right price will determine the success or failure of the syndicate he is working for means that they can command very high salaries with sums of up to £100,000 pa not being uncommon.

The second type of career available for graduates at Lloyd's is as a broker. Brokers act as agents bringing underwriters and people who want insurance together. Underwriters rely on brokers or their business because they are not allowed to deal direct. Brokers should be looking for the best deal possible for their clients. However, as the broking firms became ever more powerful so they were able to buy underwriting firms a situation which presented a conflict of interest. While they should be trying to get the best possible deal for their clients if they owned underwriting firms they might be inclined to put business in the direction which was not as cheap as it could be for the client. In order to earn their keep brokers have to go out and find the business. So to be a successful broker a person requires all the attributes of a salesman. Brokers will try to drum up business from around the world. This will not only be the more esoteric sides which other insurance companies won't cover but also re-insurance which has become increasingly important as a source of revenue. With re-insurance an insurance company which has excess risk on its book will pay another company to take on part of its risk.

Openings at Lloyd's for graduates are relatively rare. As an archetypal city institution one of the easiest ways of getting in is by being 'introduced' by somebody.

6. Merchant Banking

The gloves are off as the transatlantic giants move in for the kill

Until fairly recently the merchant banks were the gentlemen of the financial world. Forget the old Monty Python image of 'Slater-Nazi' and all that. The club atmosphere still thrived and any sharp operators who tried to bend or break the rules were severely frowned upon. Along with the club mentality came the rather restrictive recruitment patterns: no problems so long as you came from the right background (public school, Oxbridge and maybe a spot of time in the Guards) but anything less and you had your work cut out.

Nowadays, as the corporate finance kitchen begins to hot up with aggressive transatlantic rivals ready to pay top whack for the best talent, the traditional UK banks are beginning to change their ways. The meritocracy is finally having an effect on recruitment policy. What's more, some of the deals struck recently bear witness to the transatlantic influence which is increasingly gripping the City. However, the very nature of some of the transactions, particularly those concerning Guinness vis-à-vis the Distillers' takeover have begun to raise a few eyebrows. For the future, some practitioners think that there could be a marked reversal of trends back to the good old days when nobody tried to rock the boat.

Merchant banks are by no means major employers in the City. In order to stand a chance as a graduate entrant you will need a good academic track record (probably a 2.1 or better at a 'good' university). However, the subject of your degree is largely irrelevant. Unlike their American counterparts City firms, at least for the moment, are not insisting on MBAs, believing instead that on-the-job training is probably just as valid.

Another important requirement is a strong personality. If you're working in corporate finance at a merchant bank you are working in a very high profile environment which will mean plenty of client contact at the highest level combined with early responsibility. As with most other City jobs, you will be selling the bank's services and as such you're going to need a very mature and confident demeanour. If you don't feel you have the right mix of qualifications to join a merchant bank straight from university there are other routes. One of the most popular is by gaining a professional qualification. Chartered accountancy and law are the two most popular routes although MBAs are becoming increasingly important.

Corporate finance is the primary *raison d'être* for the merchant banks, and, there are a number of different activities within this ambit. First and foremost is the issuing of securities on the capital markets. When a company wants to raise more money for expansion there are essentially two routes open to it. If it is a public company it can either issue more shares or borrow the money. If it is a private company it is largely restricted to borrowing money. Either route requires a good deal of knowledge about the different ways of arranging the deals and the best ones for any particular company. This is where the merchant banks will come in. A detailed knowledge of company law and the best financing packages available for different industries are of paramount importance in such situations and is one of the reasons why quite a number of the merchant banking fraternity are either lawyers or accountants by training.

Once the company has decided on the amount of money it wants to raise it will usually approach the merchant bank who will advise on the best method. If the company is privately owned it might want to consider raising money by floating on the stock market. If so, a merchant bank has to be involved as a sponsor to the issue. It will arrange such things as underwriting and making sure that the company complies with the various Stock Exchange regulations concerning a flotation. There are usually fat fees involved for a merchant bank which can become involved with an equity flotation, particularly some of the larger ones such as British Gas and British Telecom, so the competition is fierce. However, in some instances, especially smaller flotations, costs have been pared to such an extent that the banks sometimes actually make a loss, but even running such a loss leader is still in its interests if the company is likely to be involved in a number of exciting deals in the future.

In order to get flotation business the bank will have to rely not only on its reputation but also on the quality and dedication of its staff. The larger flotations will require a great deal of time and concerted work effort which often means long hours and short weekends for the staff involved in the deal. Once a company has been floated it will still need cash from time to time and this can be arranged by issuing more shares (normally a rights issue, although other slightly more complicated methods have been used recently) or by borrowing money. The latter course of action could involve the issue of Eurobonds and this is one of the areas in which some of the larger merchant banks are now operating. Either way, before the bank gets the flotation business it will have to demonstrate to the prospective client that it has sufficient expertise in all these fields.

Thanks to the recent bout of government privatisations the raising of money via the equity market has become probably the most high profile activity of merchant banks but in hot pursuit come mergers and acquisitions. It is this side of the business which conjures up images of the more exciting if perhaps somewhat seedier side of the business, especially in the United States where corporate raiders have ruled the roost these last few years.

If a company wants to grow bigger there are essentially two ways of doing it, either organically or by acquisition. Organic growth would entail using money borrowed or generated by existing activities to expand by buying new plant and machinery, new buildings and developing new products. Acquisitions are a completely different ball game. They involve cutting out all the problems and hard work involved in building up new sections of business from scratch. The company does this by simply taking over other companies in the line of business it wants to be in. Such acquisitions can be friendly, where the board of directors of the company which is being bid for recommends that shareholders accept the takeover terms, or hostile when they don't. In either instance the merchant banks will have their role to play either for the company which is being acquired or for the one which hopes to make a successful bid. This is where the mergers and acquisitions team comes into play.

Apart from advising acquisitive companies who have identified a company suitable for takeover, some merchant banks will actually go out and find situations suitable for its client. So, for example, if X co is its client, it might spot a company which is in a similar line of business called Y co. It will then do some detailed research into Y co. This will involve finding out just how similar its activities are to X co, who holds the shares in Y co and what Y co's track record has been. Finally, it will decide how easy it would be for X co to raise the necessary finance to acquire Y co and just how feasible it would be that Y co's shareholders would accept an offer. The bank would then approach X co with its suggestions and if X co likes the idea the merchant bank will advise on financing, will help to conduct negotiations, will give advice on tactics during the bid and will help with the preparation of documents (one of the most important of which is, of course, the actual offer document where X co will lay out its terms to Y co's shareholders). All this probably seems a little cynical—the merchant bank acting like a scout hunting for quarry for its client to devour—but it certainly goes on. Those who feel some moral objection should, perhaps, not join the game. The fees, as with everything else in finance, are enormous and by generating ideas on strategy the merchant bank can gain a reputation for itself and of course generate more business as other companies become interested in its services.

Apart from these two activities merchant banks will also give general financial advice to clients. This will involve keeping the company in touch with its investors; making sure that its relationships with its main bankers are in order and that the company is getting the best possible financing arrangements; and keeping the press abreast of developments.

Graduates going straight into merchant banking can forget all about the glamorous image for at least the first few months of their training. Typically, they will either be on training courses which cover the general aspects of finance, the City and banking, or working their way around departments to try and decide which area they want to specialise in. Although the banks do have a somewhat high flying image it is important to realise that many of them will expect their graduates to sample and get to grips with some of the more tedious aspects of the business before they are allowed to become actively involved with deal making.

It should also be remembered that a lot of the glamour associated with the job is simply a reflection of its high profile nature and the fact that you are dealing with people at the highest level when you are arranging a deal for a company. Thanks to the vast amount of paperwork involved you will need to be able to pay close attention to somewhat dreary technical material for long stretches of time. This will be compounded if, as is usually the case, your office is under very strict deadlines. And to add fuel to the fire, you are invariably working on very important projects which require that everything you do is as accurate as possible. There is no room for mistakes. Once the initial deal has been struck—something which will naturally be done by senior personnel—much of the banker's task will revolve around co-ordinating the various professionals who are involved with such deals, eg accountants and lawyers. The banker will not be expected to check their work in great detail but should have a very good overall knowledge of the implications of the deal. In other words, he should know how recent tax law, for example, will affect the client company, and be expected to quiz the other professionals such as the accountants to ensure that such implications have been properly considered. Another aspect of the merchant banker's job is to make sure that any documents prepared under the bank's name comply exactly with legal and Stock Exchange requirements. This is extremely important because of the large amount of money involved in many of the deals which are undertaken. In short, the merchant banker needs to have a good eye for detail and a very firm grasp of company law and listing requirements. At the same time he or she must have the confidence to be able to discuss these requirements with other professionals.

Obviously, if you start your career in merchant banking after having gained a professional qualification you can expect to enter at a higher level and not have to put up with as much of the mundane work as graduate entrants.

Merchant banks have traditionally relied on on-the-job training to teach people how to do the job. There are no formal qualifications and most banks do not insist on your taking the Institute of Bankers examination. Another feature of the job which often appeals is that responsibility tends to be given at an early age. As with most financial occupations in the City, there is often a lot of work to be done and a shortage of staff to do all the business. So responsibility comes early and with it high remuneration packages.

Remuneration
A typical merchant banker can expect to earn around £50,000 by his mid-thirties plus substantial benefits, such as a subsidised mortgage, free life assurance bonus and a company car. For the real high flyers the remuneration packages are much higher. But there is no doubt that you have to work hard to earn your money: 10-12 hour days are the norm. You also need to have a thick skin.

One unsuccessful applicant to a big name bank was asked whether he preferred receiving or giving presents at Christmas. When he replied, 'giving' he was promptly told that he would never make a good merchant banker. Finally, bear in mind that while some of the deals are undoubtedly exciting, high profile and interesting, for the most part a merchant banker's life is like that of any other professional involved in getting the small print right and ensuring that the client doesn't get himself into trouble by not complying with the rules!

The list of major firms starts on page 98.

7. Commercial Banking

The advent of new technology has paved the way for graduates who can expect to avoid some of the more mundane aspects of the business

A career in commercial banking will entail working for one of the major high street or clearing banks such as Barclays, Lloyds, Midland, National Westminster or the Royal Bank of Scotland. The size of these banks has meant that commercial banking, rather like accountancy, has for a number of years enjoyed a cosy oligopoly. In **accountancy** the major firms dominate the audit of large companies and in banking the clearers dominate personal banking. To a large extent the clearers offer pretty much the same services, so personal customers tend not to choose their banks for strictly commercial reasons. Instead they might choose one because their parents bank there or simply because its branch is closest to home. What could be easier? The banks simply sit there and wait for the customers to come in and throw money at them.

All this is now beginning to change. In the Seventies banks tried to generate more business by looking abroad for lending opportunities. This has now begun to backfire as Third World countries—particularly in Latin America—find it increasingly difficult to repay their loans. Realising that their traditional business—lending money to the likes of you and me, and to companies—is far more lucrative and a good deal safer, the banks have now turned their attention to home. New technology means that the more routine clerical jobs such as dishing out the cash can increasingly be done by machines. The speed with which transactions can be carried out and liberalisation of the financial services industry has meant that banks can now turn their attention to a myriad other services such as insurance, estate agency and even stockbroking.

At the same time the banks have turned their gaze to the traditionally 'safe' home patch only to find that a number of interlopers have appeared on the scene. The Americans and the Japanese are over here and they want a piece of the action. Already they are starting to muscle in on the mortgage lending business traditionally dealt with by the building societies and they are now beginning to focus their attention on personal and company lending.

All this adds up to a need for higher calibre staff, especially graduates. Recently the clearing banks have become aware that in order to compete effectively they are going to need the best talent. After all, competition is not only coming from foreigners. As banks have started to offer wider and wider services so they have come increasingly to compete with each other. Innovation, marketing and selling are becoming far more important. In order to increase business banks are now having to go out and get it as opposed to sitting in their offices just waiting for it to walk through the door!

Apart from its oligopoly position commercial banking shares two other similarities with accountancy. Firstly, it is perceived to be fairly boring and secondly, you are required to take exams. The routine aspects of banking revolve around the clerical work which for many years has dominated banking. While computers are now beginning to replace this side of the business it still exists and bcause it is the nuts and bolts of the profession trainees are expected to learn it. The message is clear: don't expect to be involved in million-dollar deals within a few months of joining the bank. Instead, expect to be doing the basic clerical work such as manning the tills and filling in forms. However, on the plus side banks tend to recognise that this is not the be all and end all and, certainly at the graduate level, advancement to more responsible and interesting jobs should not take long. Additionally, the realisation by many people that banking does have more than its fair share of mundane tasks means that people do not enter the profession with rose-tinted spectacles.

During your first few years of training you are expected to pass the Institute of Bankers examinations. These exams should not be taken lightly as they can have a strong bearing on future promotion prospects. There are two stages to the exams. Graduates are exempt from Stage I. Stage II contains eight papers, all of which are directly or indirectly related to banking, such as law, accountancy, finance of international trade and economics. These exams will typically take between two and three years to pass and will, therefore, absorb a fair amount of the trainee's leisure time. Help with taking the exams will vary from bank to bank. Some offer day release courses while others expect you to attend night courses.

Nowadays the clearing banks tend to operate accelerated training programmes for graduates. This usually means that initial training will take place in London and a good deal of your time will be spent there. However, the advantage is clear in that you will avoid most of the drudgery often associated with banking. By joining one of these programmes a successful graduate should be able to take on management responsibility within three years of entry. At this level you will then become involved in the more interesting deal initiation side of things where you might be organising loans for corporate clients or, indeed, going out to find new business for the bank. Although such schemes necessarily involve a good deal of paperwork— checking figures, drafting agreements, obtaining approval etc— they do have the bonus of requiring decisions on your part. At the initiation stage you will be responsible for determining that the proposal and business plan put forward by the person wishing to borrow money are reasonable and that he or she has the necessary experience to make a success of the project. Most businesses are fairly straightforward and at first you will be dealing with relatively small and easy loan arrangements.

However, given the complex nature of some businesses there are opportunities to specialise. For example, you might become a specialist in shipping finance where the cost of new equipment, ie ships, is incredibly expensive and involves long payback periods with the possibility of a slump in the business before payback is completed. For example, during the 1970s banks who had loaned money to companies that invested in oil supertankers were faced with yet another example of how a seemingly sure-fire proposition can go disastrously wrong. In the wake of the dramatic rise in oil prices the bottom fell out of the market and many of the companies went bust.

Remuneration

Remuneration packages for commercial bankers are substantia but nowhere near as high as their counterparts in merchant banking or stockbroking. However, there are some distinc advantages. Commercial bankers are not confined to the City o London for the rest of their working lives. Opportunities exis throughout the country and career development often depend on moving between branches. The working day for a commercial banker is not usually as long as for other City professions so there is more opportunity for relaxation. The job also has a strong aspect of security about it. Unlike stockbrokers, for example, your future employment does not depend on an ever-surging stock market. Finally there are plenty of add-ons to your salary such as cheap loans, cheap mortgages and excellent pension benefits.

The list of major clearing banks starts on page 100.

8. Accountancy

Chartered Accountants

Chartered accountants are by far the largest employers in the City; accountancy may be boring but at least it's safe

If the world of finance can be compared with an iceberg, then chartered accountancy would be the great hidden mass beneath the high profile activities of Eurobond dealing, merchant banking and stockbroking. At the last count there were 102,097 chartered accountants, quietly keeping the nation's financial wheels in motion. The profession still suffers from its image of being dull and boring, having never successfully shaken off the wicked Monty Python parody, but for the graduate looking for a career in finance it needs to be taken deadly seriously.

Chartered accountancy is big business. In 1986 nearly 10 per cent of all graduates seeking employment joined the accountancy profession, making it by far the largest employer in the world of finance. The 1987 figure is expected to approach 14 per cent. Of these graduates most will go into the larger international firms which dwarf their smaller counterparts and the vast majority of them will spend at least the first three years of their professional life auditing.

Every limited company in the UK, whether it be private or public, must by law have its financial records checked by a qualified and independent professional who can be either a chartered or a certified accountant. This check is called an audit and provides the bread and butter for most firms of chartered accountants. The large international firms which employ most graduates enjoy a cosy oligopoly when it comes to audit. After all, if you're a large international company with subsidiaries worldwide you need to have an auditor with offices worldwide in order to do the job effectively. Such jobs entail massive fees and such a degree of complexity that it's very difficult for another of the large firms to muscle in. Usually, these audits have been conducted by one firm of accountants for a number of years and the only way that things are likely to change is if there is a takeover.

That's not to say that it's all sweetness and light. When it comes to smaller audits there will be a degree of competition and here the smaller accountancy firms with their lower cost structures can score points. But once the audit has been won it's usually fairly plain sailing. Companies are loath to rock the boat by changing auditors as they are well aware that such drastic action can attract unfavourable attention from shareholders and taxmen alike.

This cosy atmosphere is important to understand if you're thinking of stepping into the world of accountancy. Don't expect the cut and thrust of high finance when you join up. Deal making is very rare until you get to partner level and most of the jobs you go on will have been with the firm for donkey's years. Not much chance to impress the client or your boss by grabbing some extra business for your firm – they've seen it all before and, invariably, they've got all they want from your firm.

In fact it wasn't until comparatively recently that accountancy firms were allowed to have more than 20 partners and the old provincial atmosphere still lives on. No hi-tech offices slap bang in the heart of the City for the poor old accountant. Just some awful Sixties throw-back which is as ugly as it is functional. Forget the ulcer-inducing urgency of the City as well. Remember, the jobs are secure because every company has to be audited.

For some people this laid-back approach to the job is perfect. After all, that's what accountancy is all about, just keeping the score and letting the rest of the world get on with the game. For others this is just the sort of attitude which earns the profession its reputation for being incredibly boring. Before you think about joining up it's well worth thinking about which category you fit into.

Undergraduates looking for a career in finance will often be pointed in the direction of accountancy: the jobs are there, the qualification is highly respected and career prospects are excellent. But one of the major attractions for the graduate who is not quite sure what he wants to do with his life is that the entry requirements are really quite minimal. There's no need for specialist qualifications (arts graduates are actively encouraged) and there's none of that high pressure interviewing. Accountants are not looking for salesmen or managers, they are simply looking for personable people who can get on with the job and pass their exams.

Typically you will need grade B maths and English O level, a B and two Cs at A level and a 2.2 degree. Most accountancy firms will place greater emphasis on your O and A level achievements because of the nature of the accountancy exams. Assuming you have got the above qualifications (or you're an undergraduate and you expect to get at least a 2.2) then you should be able to secure a first interview without any real difficulty. A manager in the firm will usually sound you out in an interview which normally lasts for about half an hour. If you pass through this stage you will be asked for a second interview which will take place with a partner in the firm you intend to join. This will probably take about one hour.

Obviously, the drill will vary from firm to firm but the very fact that you can generalise to such an extent should tell you something about the profession. The big eight international firms are very much of a muchness. Don't expect to be able to haggle about your salary. In most towns the big firms meet up and agree a set salary among themselves (the only firm which doesn't join in the fun is Arthur Andersen which typically pays between 15 and 20 per cent more than the others).

What's more, the way that accountancy firms work is surprisingly similar. There are the occasional differences, but as a rule everything is departmentalised (Audit, tax, insolvency, management consultancy etc) and for most new entrants audit is all you will see. Be wary of those firms which tell you that it won't all be audit and mention that some trainees will cover other more interesting disciplines. Remember that audit is the bread and butter and the trainees are the cannon fodder. It is highly unlikely that you will escape your statutory audit duty while you are still training.

There are two aspects to a trainee accountant's job once he has joined the firm and it is vitally important to bear in mind that these don't necessarily go hand in hand. The first part of your work is the job you do from nine to five and for the vast majority this will be audit. It's important to try to come to grips with the type of work which auditing entails because, while some people take to it, for others it's the sort of drudgery which helps explain why accountancy has acquired its somewhat tarnished reputation.

Every year a company gives an account of its financial

performance (which boils down to the amount of profit it made) and the amount of its assets and liabilities–which is summarised in the balance sheet. However, a potential conflict of interest arises because the directors of a company are not necessarily shareholders (although, of course, with many smaller concerns they are one and the same). Directors, like anybody else working for the company, are ordinary employees: they are not necessarily owners of the company. However, they do have wide-ranging powers entrusted to them by the shareholders. Some directors might be tempted to take advantage of this happy state of affairs to better their lot in life. Proof that this can happen in even the largest companies has been amply demonstrated with recent widely publicised revelations about a number of major companies, including DeLorean.

The auditors' job is to try and ensure that the shareholders (who are the owners of the company) are not being ripped off by the directors (who simply run it). To this end they go in and check that the books of the company are in order. This will usually mean going to the company's offices and checking that the financial transactions have been properly and fairly recorded. In other words, you're a sort of financial Sherlock Holmes!

Before you get carried away with romantic notions of a white knight charging in on behalf of the harm done to shareholders, it's important to get things into perspective. By implication, you are checking other people's work. This has two unhappy consequences. First, people don't usually appreciate some interfering busybody fresh out of university turning up on their doorstep every year to check on a job which they have been doing for the past 20 years and second, checking other people's work can be incredibly tedious.

There's also the intriguing question of who actually deals with the auditors. Rest assured you don't get a posse of shareholders wandering around to make sure you're doing the job properly. As you've no doubt guessed, it's the directors who will deal with any matters of import. Usually you'll find a number of discrepancies on an audit but auditors aren't the types to rock the boat. So the directors and the partners of the auditing firm will reach a compromise and everyone will walk away happy. Indeed, this sort of complacency helps to explain why auditors seem to have had a rather unfortunate track record when it comes to tracing some of the large financial misdemeanours which have taken place of late.

Nevertheless there is a vast number of people for whom auditing is a great way to make a living. As time goes by the job becomes more interesting, meaningful and easy. With added responsibility you can leave aside some of the more mundane jobs and concentrate on the more interesting aspects, and within a couple of years you can expect to be running your own jobs. What's more, the job security is extremely high. Unlike a salesman's, your job isn't performance-related. In the unlikely event that your firm goes bankrupt you should have very little difficulty in transferring to another job.

But the real icing on the cake is that it's very difficult actually to assess the quality of your work. If you're a salesman your superiors can immediately see how well you have done by the amount of product which you have sold. Not so for the partner in the accountancy firm. It's difficult for him to tell whether you have checked all those transactions (unless he goes and rechecks them all himself). In fact, one of the few ways of assessing performance is by speed. This is becoming an increasingly important measure of job performance but it's easy to see where it leads. Jobs are, in some instances, not done properly. Of course, this doesn't usually matter because the books are in order. However, occasionally they aren't and increasingly in the UK companies which have suffered because of negligent auditing are turning to the courts for recourse.

The second part of the trainee's job involves studying for the exams which will secure the coveted title of chartered accountant and should virtually guarantee employment for the rest of your life. As most people are aware, this is an extremely difficult qualification to get and should under no circumstances be underestimated. It's arguable whether the technical content of the exams is particularly difficult, but the circumstances under which you have to take them are stacked against you.

Getting used to the idea that, even when you have got a job, you still have to study for exams can be difficult to adjust to, despite having been in an exam environment for several years. It's important to ask yourself how you feel about this. One of the major problems is that unless all your friends are in the same boat you're going to have to miss out on a lot of fun they're having while you slog away. It's difficult to generalise about the sort of commitment involved but you'll probably be looking at between 12 and 18 hours' study a week in your own time. That might not sound a lot but when you're doing a full-time job as well, it's amazing how quickly the time flies.

The exams themselves are fairly straightforward but there is an awful lot to learn. In this respect they are very similar to O levels and not in the least bit like taking a university degree. Some people find this aspect of the exams very difficult to come to terms with simply because they are so tedious: hardly surprising when you consider that these exams will not be that different from the old exams which articled clerks used to take.

As a graduate you will have three exams to take: graduate conversion, professional examination 1 and professional examination 2. If all goes according to plan you take one exam each year and in the third year if you pass PE 2 you are then fit to qualify as a chartered accountant.

Each exam consists of a number of papers, all of which you have to pass in one sitting. Here's how it works using the graduate conversion exam as an example. At graduate conversion level you have four papers to sit: accounts, law, economics, and quantitative techniques (statistics). If you pass all four in one sitting then you can go on to study and sit for PE 1 in a year's time. But if you fail any one of the exams you have to sit the whole lot again in six months' time. When you resit, if you again fail any of the exams, you have to resit them all again (if your contract isn't terminated by your firm!). There is only one way around sitting all the papers again. If you fail an exam by a very slim margin (within about 5 per cent of the pass mark), this is called a marginal and you only have to resit the paper you got a marginal in. But if you get two marginals then you have to retake the whole lot.

The system works like this for all the exams so it can take an awfully long time to qualify. Fortunately, the Institute of Chartered Accountants has thought about this one. Usually you'll be time barred after your third attempt at GCC or your third attempt at PE 1, and once you have passed PE 1 you must pass PE 2 within five years, or you are automatically time barred. (The rules are quite complicated but this, in essence, is what you can expect.)

Why should anyone subject themselves to such a routine for three of the best years of their lives? The answer lies in the sort of prestige which is attached to the chartered accountant's qualification. It is widely recognised as one of the best business qualifications in the UK, if not *the* best. Not only do you have the exams behind you but you also have three years of valuable work experience covering a number of companies of varying size and activity. What's more, the qualification is recognised internationally which makes it relatively easy to obtain work abroad. Apart from accountancy there are a number of different openings in the City once you are qualified, such as corporate finance or stockbroking. You are also in an excellent position to move into industry.

Remuneration

While remuneration packages are certainly quite good it must be said that accountants are the cinderellas of the finance industry when you compare their earnings with the large amounts to be earned in some City occupations. However, this must be looked at in perspective. In the first instance, City salaries have only recently started to boom and if there is a financial collapse on a par with 1974-75 not only the salaries but the jobs will soon disappear.

The second point to bear in mind is that many of the City occupations with big salaries are sales-related and thus performance-related. This is something which does not apply to accountants. Having said all that the facts speak for themselves. A graduate trainee chartered accountant in London will typically earn a starting salary of £9,000-£10,000 rising to about £15,000-£17,000 on qualification. Post-qualification, it is difficult to generalise about salaries because there are so many different options, but it must be said that some of the senior partners in the larger firms are rumoured to earn in the region of £500,000 a year.

Before you become over-excited about the earnings potential it's important to think about your reasons for choosing a career in accountancy. Some people like to take a back seat but think that by gaining a good qualification they will be able to boost themselves upwards by default. This is unlikely to work. As most university graduates are aware, the fact that you have a few letters after your name does not automatically entitle you to a job. In most cases personality is just as important, if not more important, than qualifications!

The list of major accountancy practices starts on page 100.
See also pages 63-9.

Taxation

Helping people to deal with one of the few certainties in life should keep you comfortable for the rest of yours

One way of ensuring that you will always be in demand and that, therefore, you can command a suitably high salary, is to specialise. Taxation is an obvious choice. Every year there are new amendments to the already highly complex tax laws. This means that it is very difficult for a layman to get a complete grasp of what is actually going on. In order to plan tax affairs properly a tax specialist is absolutely vital. Even very large companies will be dependent on outside expertise such as that offered by the major accounting firms to structure their finances so that they pay the minimum of tax. All of which adds up to big money for the person who is prepared to put in the hard graft.

There are essentially two ways of getting into the tax business. The first is through a chartered accountancy firm. Here you are arranging your clients' financial planning so that they pay only as little as they legally have to in tax. Clients will range from major international corporations, where the tax regimes of different countries will come into play, to individuals who are trying to cut down on their income tax liabilities. Naturally, if you work at one of the larger chartered accountancy firms it is far more likely that you will deal with corporate taxation rather than personal taxation as the fees charged will deter most individuals.

There are two ways of specialising in taxation in an accountancy firm. The most common is to qualify as an accountant and then go on to join the tax department and take the Institute of Taxation examinations. Another way which has been opened up recently is to join the tax department of a firm direct. This route is really only available in the major accountancy firms and is strictly limited to a few individuals. If you take this route then you still have to qualify as a chartered accountant but the amount of time you spend doing audit is dramatically reduced. However, there can be difficulties in specialising so early. One of the problems is that you might not get enough experience of audit ever to be able to carry out effective work as an auditor. Hand in hand with this goes the problem of not having enough audit experience to pass the exams. Nevertheless on balance it is a good way of killing two birds with one stone, both qualifying as a chartered accountant and gaining a specialisation which will make you even more marketable.

There are a number of aspects of working in taxation which differ markedly from audit. In the first instance you have a very high degree of client contact at the highest level. Businessmen and individuals alike are becoming increasingly aware that tax can have a significant impact on their finances. A slight accounting adjustment can make a big difference in the amount of tax paid. All it needs is an expert who can work his or her way around the legislative maze. This maze in itself presents some excellent opportunities for lowering the tax burden if the correct loophole can be found. So the tax expert needs to be able to work closely with a number of different types of client, to communicate effectively with them to explain the ramifications of the action which is taken and to persuade the client to act on advice given. At the same time the tax specialist needs the ability to absorb a lot of information on a continuing basis because the goalposts shift every year. Another important discipline is the ability to pay close attention to detail. The complexities of the tax laws mean that opportunities are there but you need to be able to spot them.

The second way of getting into the tax business is to join the Civil Service as a tax inspector. Here you will be sitting on the opposite side of the fence. The tax inspector has to try and ensure that citizens pay the correct amount of income tax due to the Exchequer. This will involve selecting cases which seem suspect and investigating further to find out whether the person has properly declared all the income which he or she has earned in a particular year. Similarly, companies will be investigated to ensure that the full amount of tax due has been declared and paid. Training is paid for by the Civil Service and will cover both examination training for the Civil Service taxation exams and training on such things as company accounts and law. It usually takes two years to qualify.

In your work with the tax inspectorate you will gain good experience of different aspects of taxation. Once their training is completed and they feel that they have gained enough experience a fair number of people who work for the Civil Service then 'defect' to the private sector where salaries are a good deal higher and promotion prospects are just as good. There are two advantages in taking this route. First the Civil Service usually pay more than chartered accountancy firms during training, and secondly, the trainee does not have to take the notoriously difficult chartered accountancy examinations. The drawback is that you have a particularly narrow qualification but at least you will be as good as guaranteed a job for life if you stay in the Civil Service, and as long as the tax system continues to be as complex as it is at present there will be plenty of opportunity outside the Civil Service.

One thing which is worth bearing in mind, however, is that tax inspectors are regarded in some sections of the community as being on a par with policemen. Indeed, some sections of the Inland Revenue do have a fairly heavy investigative role. However, it is fairly easy to avoid these.

Whichever route you take, specialisation in tax is likely to be a highly marketable qualification for some time to come, and along with the level of marketability come reasonably high remuneration packages.

Major companies specialising in tax work are listed on page 104.

Management Consultancy

The highly qualified 'boffins' who help industry to run more smoothly

Management consultancy is one of those catch-all occupations which covers a wide range of different disciplines and sizes of organisation. For our purposes it can be conveniently divided between the sort of services offered by the major accountancy firms and those offered by the more 'general' consultancies.

The consultancy business itself began to develop when experts in particular fields began to realise that they could not only make money by selling expertise to their employers but, equally, to other companies in the same field. As this practice became more widespread so the idea of the industry specialist became more prevalent. As companies and industries have become larger and more complex and the large multinationals have come into their own, so the need for management consultancy services has grown. Some of the more important strategic issues which now face companies need to be dealt with by outside specialists who not only know a great deal about the industry or situation under review but can also offer impartial advice.

How to Get a Highly Paid Job in the City

The 'general' management consultancies offer a wide range of services to their clients, who will tend to be very large organisations. Their aim is to help senior management to run businesses more effectively. This will involve helping them to make decisions about marketing strategy, acquisition strategy and operational strategy. So if a company called in a management consultancy firm to help it with a product launch the consultants would look at such questions as: What is the potential market size for the product? Would it be cost-effective to introduce it? What price should the product sell for? Should it be sold indirectly through retail outlets or should a direct sales force be used?, and so on. Similarly if the company were thinking of a takeover the management consultants would advise on the potential pitfalls of the takeover, the benefits, how the two companies would work together etc.

There are essentially two ways into management consultancy firms. The first is as a graduate with an MBA (Master of Business Administration) and the second is as a person who can demonstrate either a very good grasp of a specific industry or has a good experience of a number of industries. However, some of the larger firms have now started to take on graduates straight out of university. Typically, there will be a bias towards graduates with science degrees because numeracy is very important, but that in no way precludes arts graduates who can demonstrate that they are reasonably numerate. Apart from numeracy there are several key qualities which the firms are looking for, including leadership and the ability to think in a highly structured fashion.

Structured and logical thinking is very important because the consultant's work is involved with question posing and problem solving. The consultant needs to ask the question: What would happen if a company went ahead with a certain plan which it has? This will involve finding the appropriate information on the particular company or industry, sifting through it and identifying the most important and relevant parts. This will then be arranged into a logic tree and the relevant conclusion drawn.

On-the-job training for a direct graduate entrant will usually involve working in a team for a particular client. The team will be given specific parts of the problem to look at and will be left to their own devices to gather the relevant information necessary to solve the problem and to draw a conclusion. The next step is for the team to construct a plan which will both help the client and appeal to him. The person in charge of the team then has to make sure that the proposals are properly carried out so that the client will obtain the maximum benefit.

Given this quite wide brief confidence is a key factor for the consultant because in a number of instances he or she is not going to have specific knowledge of the industry in which the client is operating. However, the clients are bound to be involved and the consultant has to be able to instil them with belief in his or her ability to solve the company's problems.

Direct graduate entrants to this sort of management consultancy firm will, after a period of two years, usually be expected to attend business school. In some cases firms have their own in-house training but for the most part they will want the graduate to obtain some detailed formal training in the skills which are necessary to the job. Here they will go through an accelerated development programme covering a number of different case studies. At the same time the person gets the opportunity to meet a number of people from different backgrounds and to decide exactly whether management consultancy is right for them. Most of the larger consultancy firms will provide you with some form of financial help for your MBA tuition fees by way of a loan and some will pay the lot. If you then rejoin the firm the loan is written off but if you go elsewhere you are obliged to repay it. Typically, the favoured business schools will be in the United States—eg Harvard or Wharton—although it is possible to attend one closer to home in Paris (INSEAD) or London.

Once you have gone through this process and become a fully fledged consultant there are openings throughout the world either in the firm that you are working for or in other companies. The important point is that the qualification is highly transferable and sought after worldwide.

You will also be able to work in a wide range and variety of industries, all of which require experts to help run them. Major chartered accountancy firms too are now beginning to offer management consultancy services to their clients. As the bread-and-butter audit work becomes increasingly price-competitive so the profits earned are gradually being squeezed. This has led the major accountancy firms to look at other areas such as management consultancy where they can offer a good service to their clients and make very sizeable profits. With the client base already set up—through audit work—and the ability to charge very high fees (upwards of £700 a day per person) this has now become one of the major growth areas for accountants.

High fees mean that it is most unlikely that you will be able to move straight from university into management consultancy at an accountancy firm. Usually the only graduates to be taken straight on would have degrees in either computing or economics. That way they can do effective work in the backroom and be brought forward after a few years' training. You would therefore normally move into consultancy after first qualifying as a chartered accountant.

The major accountancy firms which have become involved in consultancy have initially simply concentrated on the systems implementation side of things with particular emphasis on data processing and new technology. So if a client wishes to implement a new system the accountancy firm will tell them how to do it in the most cost-effective and efficient way. The accountancy firm will in many instances devise the whole system so that the correct information flows are in place. These will then be checked to make sure that they work effectively. Obviously, over the past few years this particular side of the business has grown as new technology has made advanced computerised systems available to all but the smallest companies. Faced with the bewildering display of computer technology on the market many companies have needed someone to turn to for independent advice. One of the most natural sources is the company auditor, who has a wide range of knowledge in different industries, has probably looked after the company for a number of years and understands the company's system requirements.

In short, the 'general' management consultancy firms will look at strategic issues such as should I do X, Y or Z? This will cover a wide range of issues from marketing and sales to acquisition strategies. On the other hand, the accountancy firms involved in management consultancy will normally concentrate on implementing systems and not so much on advising the client on a particular strategy.

However, it is true to say that this is beginning to change. Some of the larger accountancy firms have started to appreciate that over the next few years one of their major growth areas will be non-audit services, such as management consultancy, and with this in mind they have started to beef up their services. Like the 'general' consultancies they will offer a surprisingly wide range of services focused upon developing an overall strategy for a business or organisation. This will involve examining the impact of political issues, economic circumstances, current and possible future competition in the market-place in which the business is operating, ecological factors etc. Apart from this general planning, consultancies will also focus on specific issues such as employment strategy. This would include looking at levels of remuneration within an organisation and any anomalies, bonuses offered and comparative rates of pay within the same industry and similar sized organisations.

Remuneration
As with 'general' consultancies, working for a major accountancy firm will give you the opportunity to work around the world. Remuneration packages are usually very high with typical pay scales running at between £25,000 and £30,000 pa for a consultant with two to three years' experience. Pay is so high largely because of the highly complex nature of the work and because of the level of education necessary to do it effectively.

Major management consultancy firms are listed on page 105.

9. Headhunters

With everyone swapping jobs, the recruitment specialists are having a field day

Headhunters are more properly called recruitment consultants. They find specialised staff on behalf of clients, and receive a fee for their services, based on the salary of the hired personnel. This field is growing very fast within the City, as expanding firms increasingly demand able and experienced staff from a smallish pool of potential applicants. Headhunters operate at middle to senior staff levels, since junior recruits are more cheaply and easily hired through conventional wanted ads or via colleges and universities. The lucrative headhunting work is right at the top, where chief executives and directors are chosen. Normally, only a few people are suitable for the position. They have to be approached in a discreet manner by a third party, and this is where the headhunter's relative anonymity is vital. Usually, headhunting fees are substantial, often £10,000 for finding a high ranking individual, but they are payable only on success—if the headhunter fails to fill a slot with a suitable person, he earns nothing.

Traditionally, headhunting was carried out by experienced and senior individuals operating quietly within small firms and partnerships. That has now changed. With the explosive growth of salaries in the financial world, the increasing amount of job movement among senior staff, and the increasing level of area specialisation, the demand for headhunting services has soared. The period leading up to big bang in the City was one of frenetic activity for the good recruitment consultants, as major new international players from America, Europe, and Japan moved into UK investment banking and stockbroking. All these foreign outfits wanted experienced, local staff. Movement of the rated people from company to company became extraordinary—and with it the fees earned by the headhunters. Several of the more important headhunting groups merged or were bought up by larger concerns in advertising and PR. The business is extremely high margin, although it depends a lot on the relative prosperity of the job market in which it operates. If the City goes into a downturn (an unlikely possibility in the near future), headhunters will be among those first to suffer.

Recruitment organisations in the City have thus become more typical in their management structure as the market has boomed. The big groups now have active graduate recruitment schemes, although they find most of their staff from the ranks of experienced City slickers—bankers, accountants, brokers and the like. Since a good headhunter must understand exactly the vacancy to be filled, the qualities the employer is looking for, and the various choices facing any potential recruit, a thorough knowledge of the job and the companies is necessary. Often someone moves from a specific discipline, say Eurobonds, to recruit Eurobond dealers and traders—their expertise and contacts will be invaluable.

There are two different sides to the job. One is dealing with the client; the other is talking with recruits. For major job prospects, involving a big salary package (and consequently a handsome fee: 25 per cent of the first year's wages is not uncommon), a detailed analysis will be undertaken of the exact specifications and requirements of the task. The headhunter will talk to all the people concerned with filling the vacancy at their offices, to better see who might be just right to fill the gap. He will prepare a documentary job specification, to be approved by the client; and he will then proceed to search through his files to see if any names already on his books might be worth approaching.

There then follows a considerable amount of interviewing, always person to person, since a potential recruit is unlikely to want to talk aloud about such a sensitive matter over the phone in the middle of the office! Usually the headhunter will screen a considerable number of possibles by finding out just how happy they are in their present role. If they are quite content, it may prove extremely difficult and ultimately pointless trying to tempt them away just for cash.

Headhunters are normally experts at salary, pay and bonus levels, and will certainly advise their clients on the appropriate amount of money needed to secure a decent candidate. The individual headhunters normally work off highly commission-geared salaries, which reflect their success at filling vacancies. The most able people in the business certainly earn £250,000 per annum and more. Firms do not baulk at paying out these colossal fees if they find a highly valuable member of staff, who might well generate business worth more than this in a matter of months. Usually, a proportion of the fee is repayable in the event that a recruit leaves quite soon after joining. It is part of a headhunter's job to try and ensure that these individuals are weeded out early in the selection process.

The job can be frustrating in that people may haggle and debate about joining a firm for many weeks, and then decide not to take the job offer—or go somewhere else entirely. Alternatively, the client may suddenly decide after weeks of painstaking research by the headhunter that they are to promote from within. Nevertheless, a headhunter who successfully places a candidate within a firm can be assured of two friends: the client and the candidate. Frequently, a headhunter will end up being used by an individual who was originally placed within a firm by the same headhunter. Most business is obtained by word of mouth recommendation, and personal reputation built up by intelligent placements.

Competition in the industry, especially City and financial recruitment, has hotted up considerably. One of the attractions for anyone thinking of entering this field is the ease with which it is possible to establish your own operation—all that is required is a phone and an interviewing room. Since entrepreneurial types are drawn to the job anyhow, there are numerous break-aways from the big firms, when senior staff will take their own list of contracts within clients and securities firms. These split-ups can be acrimonious—as can the attitude from a potential recruit's employers, when they find he or she is talking to a headhunter.

A good headhunter needs to be outgoing and friendly, and above all an attentive listener. They should be astute judges of character, and see through the sometimes artificial personalities people project in interviews. They need persuasive skills, in order to entice a client to offer them an assignment, and to coax a potential candidate to take a job offer seriously. An ability to read a CV realistically—and perhaps even help in preparing one—is an advantage. An ear for gossip, to hear where the big management reshuffles are going on, and where vacancies might crop up, or where people are unhappy and might welcome an approach, is also valuable.

10. Financial Public Relations

Public relations covers a multitude of sins ranging from acting as a post box—simply disseminating information—to organising a complete media strategy which it is hoped will give your client maximum exposure and enhance its reputation with the world at large. Financial public relations is a profitable offshoot of the industry, which has only really come into its own over the past ten years.

Until relatively recently financial PR was a very leisurely, almost laid back, profession. Introducing a journalist to the chairman of your client company over gin and tonic down at the club was very much par for the course. In those days the PR firms really did act as post boxes. Information was sent to them from the client company which would then be turned into a press release and sent off to the appropriate journalists. This would then be chased up to see if they would publish the piece but that was usually the end of the story.

All this has changed over the past few years. Now PR companies have come to realise that they can increasingly dominate the news and to some extent dictate how it is written. This has become more and more important in the financial world where billion-pound takeovers are not uncommon. In line with this comes the fact that in most instances these are hostile takeovers where a battle will be fought for ultimate control of the company. Under such circumstances an ability to manipulate the supposedly independent press is absolutely essential.

How does it work? Basically, financial PR companies usually act for public companies who want to maintain a high profile in the press. Usually these will be the larger concerns but nowadays even very small quoted companies are beginning to appreciate the importance of having a high profile both in the City and with the public at large. The reason is quite simple: for a company which is hoping to grow by acquisition—ie taking over other companies—its share price is vitally important. By employing a good PR firm or by issuing shares to raise cash for expansion a fair share of press coverage is ensured, thus attracting investor interest. Until a few years ago financial PR firms used to carry out their trade on an *ad hoc* basis. You simply told the journalist the story, then he decided whether to run it or not.

All that has now changed. PR companies with major clients on their books realised that they had control of some of the hottest stories well in advance of any journalist. By dangling a few carrots every now and again it has become possible for PR companies to make sure that when they want a story published, in it goes. The PR firm then becomes trapped in a virtuous circle. It can dominate the news so it gets bigger and bigger clients on its books. Because it has bigger and bigger clients it has access to better and better stories. The journalists need these stories so they are prepared to play the game and help the PR companies out, so long as they get the occasional good feed.

As with financial journalism, getting into PR works on a fairly impromptu basis. There is an awful lot of writing involved so PR firms will be on the look-out for people with literary ability. This is all the more important because the stuff you are writing—press releases for example—will have to be eyecatching; otherwise it stands a reasonable chance of being confined to the waste-paper bin by the recipient. Press releases are simply brief résumés describing a product which a company has launched or a news item concerning the company. In addition to writing press releases PR firms will often write reports to clients on what they should or shouldn't be doing and the PR officer will also field enquiries from journalists.

Given these criteria there are a number of routes into PR. One of the most common is to move in from journalism. PR companies on the whole can afford to pay more than trade magazines and in some instances more than national newspapers. So when journalists tire of the routine of daily deadlines they often drift into PR. People who work in the City are also tempted in occasionally by the reasonably high salaries and, in the past, by the fairly relaxed lifestyle.

Of course, one of the best ways of ensuring that your client obtains maximum exposure is to arrange a good press conference or day out. Ordinary punters will often marvel at the prices which are paid for tickets at 'society' events such as Wimbledon. The reason is very simple: in a lot of instances PR firms snap them up. After all, if you take a party of hacks to Wimbledon for the day and fill them to the gills with champagne and strawberries, they are hardly likely to forget the company which was so generous and any subsequent reporting can reasonably be expected to be complimentary. So organising these events will take up a considerable part of PR time.

In order to succeed at PR you need a number of qualities. You have to be a natural salesperson, sociable and thick skinned. Usually, if you're trying to sell a story to a journalist over the phone you will be competing with a number of equally 'good' stories. There is only a limited amount of editorial space to fill and that is what you are fighting for. So you need to be persuasive. When you hold a press conference you have to play host or hostess: introducing journalists to your clients and vice versa and generally making sure that the momentum of the occasion is maintained.

Remuneration

Salaries vary from company to company but a PR officer in his mid-thirties can reasonably expect to earn £25,000-£30,000 plus a car. Obviously, if he has been enticed away from a national newspaper then the salary will be even higher. In the past, one of the major advantages of the job was the fairly relaxed lifestyle. Nowadays, as deals in the City have become much larger and increasingly important, so the business has become far more cutthroat.

The list of major firms starts on page 106.

11. Financial Journalism

Financial journalists are in many respects the mouthpieces of the City. They not only communicate the news to investors outside the City but also act as an information exchange for people within it. This role has become increasingly important as careers within the square mile become more and more specialised. Equally important is the perceived independence of journalists. From this position—which is unique in the City—they can wield an enormous amount of influence. Companies' share prices can often be affected by the write-ups they receive in newspapers and magazines, as can the outcome of takeover bids and the success or otherwise of financial products such as unit trusts. There are essentially four types of financial journalism. By far the most common are City or stock market journalism and personal finance journalism. City journalism revolves around the 2000+ quoted companies on the Stock Exchange. The journalist is concerned with interesting developments in these companies— changes in management, new products, major shareholders etc—and the future prospects of the company which will naturally affect the share price. In fact, for the most part this type of journalism can be boiled down to the assessment of a company's share price: is it too high, too low or about right?

Until a few years ago there was a fairly well defined path into City journalism. Magazines such as *Investor's Chronicle, Investor's Review* and the *Investor's Guardian* took on trainees, usually from university. Such publications provided not only fertile training grounds but also invaluable ways of building up a network of contacts. Of these three publications only the *Investor's Chronicle* remains and although it does take on the occasional graduate, it seems increasingly to be looking for people with City experience either as merchant bankers, stockbrokers or possibly accountants. In fact, training or working in the City before you become a journalist is now becoming a very popular choice. I this doesn't appeal then there is always the time-honoured route of joining a local newspaper and working your way up from there. In short, unlike most other occupations in the City, the route into financial journalism is very *ad hoc* and you will find a number of backgrounds ranging from ex-crime reporters to ex-stockbrokers.

City journalism can be neatly sub-divided into two categories: periodicals and magazines—including newsletters—and national daily or Sunday newspapers. Magazines will concentrate on features more than news items. However, there will inevitably be a certain amount of news and financial analysis of companies, usually in the form of an assessment of the latest results or, especially in the case of newsletters, investment recommendations in the form of share tipping. On the other hand, newspapers will naturally focus more on news items although, for the Sunday papers, share tipping and longish features will also come into play.

For most journalists the major goal will be to land a job on one of the national newspapers. Obviously, it is difficult to generalise about how long this will take but the best should be able to progress from periodicals to nationals in about two or three years. Typically, a city journalist will join a national newspaper as a company news reporter. Before you join you should be able to demonstrate that you understand the basics of company reports and accounts and that you can interpret the figures which underlie them. When a company reports its figures you should be able to ask the right kinds of sensible question to be able to find out just how well or badly it has really done and whether it is going to do well in the future (again coming back to the main question of what is the right share price). If you can demonstrate this and show that you have a basic understanding of a number of different industries, then you are classic fodder for the company news section of the dailies which cover the City.

Joining at this level you will spend the first year or so doing little more than attending press conferences and re-writing press releases with a good deal of phoning round—usually stockbrokers—to find out what the City opinion is of a company's announcement, be it yearly results, an acquisition or a new product or management. The City here is in a very real sense talking to itself, as journalists will rely on the professionals to provide comment on a company's performance.

This training ground is invaluable as it will allow you to build up your contacts within the City. Of course, the better your contacts the better the quality of information you get, which in turn leads to better stories and a better reputation for yourself. After a few years you will have developed contacts among stockbrokers, bankers and the companies which you have covered. Equally important will be the contacts you build up at PR agencies as these firms usually have access to the best information. As you build up special links with PR firms so you will get favoured invitations and early leaks. At the same time your all-important list of contacts will not only be getting larger but more influential. After about five or six years you will start to find that some of the people you started with or knew at university or who were early contacts have grown up with you and have become deal initiators. This means that they have better information to give you and you can start to break your own stories. At the same time you become an information exchange in your own right. Obviously, when you make a contact you want information and in the same way they often want information from you. When you become a two-way source of information the terms of trade automatically change. Instead of your phoning up and pleading for information you in effect become equals. You can give your contact information, your contact can give you information and the relationship is exactly balanced. As this process goes on so you become a self-starter. With a good solid core of valuable contacts with whom you are quite friendly, it is much less of a hassle to get a story and in many respects the stories come to you through simply meeting your contacts for a drink or phoning up and chatting to them.

At this stage in your development you will be ready for Sunday journalism. This side of the business relies heavily on getting exclusive news stories for which you need to have impeccable contacts. One way of doing this is to build up your contacts at PR firms. Indeed, there is an increasing feeling among some old hands that Sunday papers are in many instances totally dominated by PR firms who can provide the exclusive stories which the journalists thrive on (see the chapter on PR page 73). Another way of getting good information is either to build up your contacts in the City so you know a number of deal makers, or alternatively to become friendly with a number of high-profile company directors who sit on the boards of a number of public companies. By taking this route you can develop a relationship which is mutually beneficial. If the director is involved in a deal for which he needs maximum favourable publicity you will provide it. In return you will receive the occasional titbit of exclusive information which only people at the highest level of a company have access to.

For those people who hate getting up in the morning journalism is just the ticket! On a daily newspaper you will usually get into work at around 10-10.30 am and a morning conference will be held. You will be given stories to work on and deadlines will be set for between 5 and 5.30 pm. One of the main criticisms now being levelled at the business is that increasingly the news side of financial journalism is being controlled by the news producers rather than the journalists. Press conferences are far more common than they used to be and these are in many cases designed to set the agenda rather than to disseminate information. By calling a press conference you can determine what the press should be given and restrict your information to just that. This prevents the journalist from wandering footloose and finding out exactly what he wants to find out. The scope of what you report on will also be severely curtailed by both the amount of space available and the number of standard announcements which have to be covered (such as the results for major companies like BT or ICI). So although there is a huge investigative role to be played in financial journalism it is becoming less and less evident. Most of the information is publicly available and any news which is leaked will soon be in the public domain. PR firms are increasingly dominating the business and they like reporters to play their game. What's more, in most cases there just isn't the time to do proper investigative reports which will produce concrete results.

Aside from City work, the other most common type of journalism is in personal finance. This aspect of the business deals with such things as unit trusts, taxation, insurance, mortgages and pensions. As such it is far more product-driven than City journalism. Instead of looking at companies and deciding whether they are worth investing in or not, the personal finance reporter will be looking at products such as a new unit trust or a new life assurance scheme and determining whether this offers good value and to whom it offers the best value. This side of financial journalism tends to be far easier to break into. There are a number of openings on trade papers which will often take on graduates. Usually this sort of publication will concentrate on one side of the personal finance market such as pensions or insurance. While this might be a little narrow at first it is important to do the basic training because specialisation is an important aspect of this game. If you can set yourself up as a specialist in one particular area you will always have your bread-and-butter earnings while you build up your knowledge of other areas. On the national and Sunday newspapers the personal finance 'club' is a fairly small band of journalists which it is very difficult to break into. Many have established themselves as experts in a particular field and operate as freelancers working for a number of different publications. Nevertheless there are openings and someone with sufficient drive and a couple of years' experience should at least be able to do freelance work for one of the major papers.

Aside from the mainstream City and personal finance journalists come in a mixture of different types. A few journalists, no doubt aided by the success of *Euromoney* magazine, have carved themselves a niche covering the Euromarkets. There are also a large number of general business journalists who will cover such things as management strategy, product launches and marketing strategy. Finally, there are the industrial journalists who cover industrial relations, union agreements etc.

A strong liver and a good memory are the two vital ingredients for a financial journalist. The financial services industry is growing rapidly and the participants are prepared to pay well to ensure that their products get the maximum favourable exposure. Journalists will normally be asked to attend at least one press conference a week and this will inevitably involve a certain amount of eating and drinking. This can range from tea and biscuits at the company's offices to a day trip to Henley or the Derby with champagne flowing freely all day.

In order to be truly effective and to succeed in the business the journalist needs to be the sociable sort who can mix in City circles and develop useful and long-lasting contacts. This means being able to hold your end up in conversation and to get on with a wide cross section of individuals.

Remuneration

Earnings for journalists do vary quite widely. On trade papers salaries tend to be quite low, starting at around £10,000 pa. However, it is relatively easy to double this by doing freelance work. On national newspapers salaries tend to be a lot higher. People with a name in the business at the City or investment editor level will be able to command salaries over £50,000 while their number twos, threes and even fours should be able to earn upwards of £35,000 pa. In addition, freelance work is a lot easier to get and very lucrative.

There tends to be something of a two-way traffic between financial journalism and the City. While a number of financial journalists will have previously worked in the City, some people who work in stockbroking, PR or merchant banking will have previously worked as financial journalists. In fact, a background in financial journalism tends to help most City careers because it both gives a good overall view of the City and helps build up contacts.

The list of major financial publications starts on page 107.

Part 2: Targeting the Job

Jobhunter's Directory

The following list, compiled in June 1987, is designed to help you start on your job hunt here and now. In it we have given a large number of major firms and companies operating in the financial services industry. As things are constantly changing, we would recommend that you get in touch with the firms prior to sending your application to ensure that you are writing to the correct person.

With the recent upheavals in the City there are quite a number of companies and firms which carry out a wide range of activities (a bit like a financial supermarket). We have listed these outfits under each of the activities it carries. While this involves a degree of repetition it should help to avoid confusion.

Although the list is designed to be as comprehensive as possible there will no doubt be firms or companies which we have omitted. Obviously, this should not preclude them from your job search!

Capital Markets — Eurobounds Etc

Bache Securities (UK)
9 Devonshire Square
London EC2M 4HP
01-283 9166
Contact – Miss D Howell

Bank of America International
1 Watling Street
London EC4P 4BX
01-634 4000
Contact – Mr A Tucker

Bank of Montreal Capital Markets
Bucklersbury House
9 Queen Victoria Street
London EC4N 4XN
01-236 1010
Contact – Personnel Department

Bank of Tokyo International
20–24 Moorgate
London EC2R 6DH
01-628 3000
Contact – Mrs E Penycote

Bankers Trust International
Dashwood House
69 Old Broad Street
London EC2P 2EE
01-726 4141
Contact – Mr J Adshead,
Vice President of London Personnel

Banque Paribas Capital Markets
33 Wigmore Street
London W1H 0BN
01-355 2000
Contact — Mr M Forrester

Baring Brothers & Co
8 Bishopsgate
London EC2N 4AE
01-283 8833
Contact – Miss E Williams

Baring Securities
Lloyds Chambers
Portsoken Street
London E1 8DF
01-621-1500
Contact – Mrs K Curran

Bear Sterns International
9 Devonshire Square
London EC2M 4YL
01-626 5656
Contact – Personnel Department

Chase Investment Bank
Woolgate House
Coleman Street
London EC2P 2HD
01-726 5000
Contact – Personnel Department

Chemical Bank International
180 Strand
London WC2R 1ET
01-379-7474
Contact – Mrs J Masters

Citicorp Investment Bank
335 Strand
London WC2R 1LS

01-836 1230
Contact – Ms S Day

**Credit Suisse First Boston
Securities**
22 Bishopsgate
London EC2N 4BQ
01-634 3000
Contact – Personnel Department

Daiwa Europe
Condor House
14 St Paul's Churchyard
London EC4M 8BD
01-248 8080
Contact – Mr G Stevenson

**Dean Witter Capital Markets
International**
56 Leadenhall Street
London EC3A 2BH
01-480 8500
Contact – Miss S Patterson

Deutsche Bank Capital Markets
150 Leadenhall Street
London EC3V 4RJ
01-283 0933/4971
Contact – Mr R Austin-Cooper

DKB International
Garden House
18 Finsbury Circus
London EC2M 7BP
01-638 9433
Contact – Mr A Avenell

**Drexel Burnham Lambert
Securities**
82–86 Fenchurch Street
London EC2M 1BE
01-920 9797
Contact – Mrs H McKenzie

EBC Amro Bank Ltd
10 Devonshire Square
London EC2M 4HS
01-621 0101
Contact – Mr K Wood

First Chicago Ltd
First Chicago House
90 Long Acre
London WC2E 9RB
01-379 3414
Contact – Mrs M Farrer

Robert Fleming Securities
25 Copthall Avenue
London EC2R 7DR
01-638 5858
Contact – Mr F Smith

Fuji International Finance
101 Moorgate
London EC2M 6TQ
01-638 1421
Contact – Mr K Cripps

Goldman Sachs International Cprn
5 Old Bailey
London EC4V 4DB
01-248 6464
Contact – Mr A Smith

Hambros Bank
41 Bishopsgate
London EC2P 2AA
01-588 2851
Contact – Personnel Department

Hill Samuel & Co
100 Wood Street
London EC2P 2AJ
01-628 8011
Contact – Personnel Department

EF Hutton & Co (London)
Princess House
152–156 Upper Thames Street
London EC4R 3UH
01-623 0900/0800
Contact – Personnel Director

BJ International
Bucklersbury House
Queen Victoria Street
London EC4N 8HR

01-236 1090
Contact – Mr I Matheson

Kidder Peabody Securities
107 Cheapside
London EC2V 6DD
01-480 8200
Contact – Personnel Director

Kleinwort Benson
20 Fenchurch Street
London EC3P 3DB
01-623 8000
Contact – Personnel Department

Manufacturers Hanover Ltd
7 Princes Street
London EC2P 2AX
01-600 5666
Contact – Personnel Department

Merrill Lynch International
3 Newgate Street
London EC1A 7DA
01-382 8980
Contact – Mr K Robinson

Samuel Montagu & Co
10 Lower Thames Street
London EC3R 6AE
01-260 9000
Contact – Mr J Young

Morgan Grenfell & Co
23 Great Winchester Street
London EC2P 2AX
01-588 4545
Contact – Mr P Lefevre

J P Morgan
Morgan House
PO Box 161
1 Angel Court
London EC2R 7AE
01-600 2300
Contact – Personnel Department

Morgan Stanley International
Kingsley House
1A Wimpole Street

London W1M 7AA
01-709 3000
Contact – Mr P Mills

Nomura International
24 Monument Street
London EC2R 8AJ
01-283 8811
Contact – Mr M Brookes

Orion Royal Bank
1 London Wall
London EC2Y 5JX
01-600 6222
Contact – Mr D Blacker

Paine Webber International Trading
1 Finsbury Avenue
London EC2M 2PA
01-377 0055/6533
Contact – Mr G Soper

Phillips & Drew
120 Moorgate
London EC2M 6XP
01-628 4444
Contact – Mrs S Mew

Salomon Brothers International
Victoria Plaza
111 Buckingham Palace Road
London SW1W 0SB
01-721 2000
Contact – Mr M West

J Henry Schroder Wagg & Co
120 Cheapside
London EC2V 6DS
01-382 6000
Contact – Miss S Cox

Security Pacific Hoare Govett
Security Pacific House
4 Broadgate
London EC2M 7LE
01-601 0101
Contact – Personnel Department

Shearson Lehman Brothers International
9 Devonshire Square
London EC2M 4YL
01-626 2525
Contact – Personnel Department

Smith Barney Harris Upham International
18 Finsbury Circus
London EC2M 7SAQ
01-588 6040
Contact – Mr S Vivaldis,
Managing Director

Société Générale Strauss Turnbull
3 Moorgate Place
London EC2R 6HR
01-638 5699
Contact – Personnel Department

Standard Chartered Merchant Bank
33–36 Gracechurch Street
London EC3V 0AX
01-623 8711
Contact – Mrs J Phillip

Sumitomo Finance International
5th Floor
107 Cheapside
London EC2V 6HA
01-606 3001
Contact – Mrs F Williams

Swiss Bank Corporation Internationl
Three Keys House
130 Wood Street
London EC2V 6AQ
01-600 0844
Contact – Mr D Packham

Union Bank of Switzerland (Securities)
Stock Exchange Building
Old Broad Street
London EC2N 1EY

01-588 6666
Contact – Personnel Department

Warburg Securities
1 Finsbury Avenue
London EC2M 2PA
01-280 2990
Contact – Personnel Department

Wood Gundy
30 Finsbury Square
London EC2A 1SB
01-628 4030
Contact – Personnel Department

Yamaichi International (Europe)
Finsbury Court
111–117 Finsbury Pavement
London EC2A 1EQ
01-638 5599
Contact – Mr J Smith

Stockbrokers

Alexanders Laing & Cruickshank
Piercy House
Copthall Avenue
London EC2R 7BT
01-588 2800
Contact – Personnel Department

Barclays de Zoete Wedd
Ebbgate House
2 Swan Lane
London EC4R 3TS
01-623 2323
Contact – Mr P Thompson

Bell Lawrie Ltd
PO Box 8
Erskine House
68–73 Queen Street
Edinburgh EH2 4AE
Contact – Mr Mackie

James Capel & Co
James Capel House
6 Bevis Marks
London EC3A 7JQ
01-621 0011
Contact – Personnel Department

Capel Cure Myers
65 Holborn Viaduct
London EC1A 2EU
01-236 5080
Contact – Miss P Nickalls

Cazenove
12 Tokenhouse Yard
London EC2R 7AN
01-588 2828
Contact – Personnel Department

Chase Manhattan Securities
Woolgate House
Coleman Street
London EC2P 2HD
01-726 5000
Contact – Personnel Department

County Securities Ltd
Drapers Gardens
12 Throgmorton Avenue
London EC2P 2ES
01-382 1000
Contact – Miss E Heath, Personnel
Department, 21st Floor West

Credit Suisse Buckmaster & Moore
18th & 19th Floors
The Stock Exchange
London EC2P 2JT
01-588 2868
Contact – Personnel Department

Greenwell Montagu
Bow Bells House
Bread Street
London EC4M 9EL
01-236 2040
Contact – Mrs V Murphy

Greig Middleton & Co
78 Old Broad Street
London EC2M 1JE
01-920 0481
Contact – Personnel Department

Grenfell & Colegrave
55–61 Moorgate
London EC2R 6DR

01-628 6044
Contact — Personnel Department

Henderson Crosthwaite Ltd
32 St Mary-at-Hill
London EC3 3AJ
01-623 9333
Contact – Mr E Hathorn

Henry Cooke Lumsden
PO Box 369
1 King Street
Manchester M60 3AH
061-834 2332
Contact – Office Manager

Hoare Govett Ltd
4 Broadgate
London EC2M 7LE
01-601 0101
Contact – Personnel Department

Kitcat & Aitken
The Stock Exchange
London EC2N 1HB
01-588 6280
Contact – Personnel Department

Kleinwort Grieveson Securities
PO Box 560
20 Fenchurch Street
London EC3P 3DB
01-623 8000
Contact – Personnel Department

Laurence Prust
Basildon House
7–11 Moorgate
London EC2R 6AH
01-606 8811
Contact – Mr J Arthur

Montagu Loebl Stanley
31 Sun Street
London EC2M 2QP
01-377 9242
Contact – Personnel Department

Panmure Gordon
9 Moorfields
Highwalk

London EC2Y 9DS
01-638 4010
Contact – Personnel Department

Penney Easton & Co
PO Box 112
24 George Square
Glasgow G2 1EB
041-248 2911
Contact – Mr W Aitchison

Phillips & Drew
120 Moorgate
London EC2M 6XP
01-628 4444
Contact – Mrs S Mew

Quilter Goodison
Garrard House
31–45 Gresham Street
London EC2V 7LH
01-600 4177
Contact – Mr D Weeks

Raphael Zorn
10 Throgmorton Avenue
London EC2N 2DP
01-628 4000
Contact – Mr D Betts

Rowe & Pitman
c/o Mercury Group
33 King William Street
London EC4R 9AF
01-280 2222
Contact — Mr G Woods

Savory Miln Ltd
New City Court
20 St Thomas Street
London SE1 9RP
01-638 1212
Contact – Mr P Cole

Scrimgeour Vickers
PO Box 21
20 Copthall Avenue
London EC2R 7JS
01-600 7595
Contact – Personnel Department

Albert E Sharp
Edmund House
12 Newhall Street
Birmingham B3 3ER
021-236 5801
Contact – Personnel Department

Shearson Lehman Brothers Ltd
1 Broadgate
London EC2M 7HA
01-601 0011
Contact – Graduate Recruitment
Officer

Sheppards
1 London Bridge
London SE1 9QU
01-378 7000
Contact – Personnel Department

Smith Keen Cutler
Exchange Buildings
Stephenson Place
Birmingham B2 4NN
021-643 9977
Contact – Personnel Department

Strauss Turnbull & Co Ltd
3 Moorgate Place
London EC2R 6HR
01-638 5699
Contact – Mr R S Betts

Wood Mackenzie & Co
100 Wood Street
London EC2P 2AJ
01-600 3600
Contact – Mr D Boath

Commodity/Financial Futures Brokers

Arbuthnot Latham Bank
131 Finsbury Pavement
Moorgate
London EC2A 1AY
01-280 8400
Contact – Personnel Department

Australia & New Zealand Banking Group
Minerva House
Montagu Close
London SE1 9DH
01-280 3100
Contact – Mr J Birch

Bache Securities Ltd
9 Devonshire Square
London EC2M 4HP
01-283 9166
Contact – Miss D Howell

Julius Baer International Ltd
Bevis Marks House
Bevis Marks
London EC3A 7NE
01-623 4211
Contact – Mr A Burns

The Bank of Tokyo Ltd
20–24 Moorgate
London EC2R 6DH
01-638 1271
Contact – Mr A Breeze

Banque Paribas Capital Markets Ltd
33 Wigmore Street
London W1H 0BN
01-355 2000
Contact – Mr M Forrester

James Capel (Financial Futures) Ltd
James Capel House
6 Bevis Marks
London EC3A 7JQ
01-621 0011
Contact – Personnel Department

Cargill UK Ltd
3 Shortlands
Hammersmith
London W6 8RT
01-741 9090
Contact – Mr A McDonald

Charterhouse Bank Ltd
1 Paternoster Row
St Paul's
London EC4M 7DH
01-248 4000
Contact – Mr J McCarthy

Chase Manhattan Bank
Woolgate House
Coleman Street
London EC2P 2HD
01-726 5000
Contact – Personnel Department

Chemical Bank Internationl
180 Strand
London WC2R 1ET
01-379 7474
Contact – Personnel Department

Citifutures Ltd
45–50 Cannon Street
London EC4
01-248 2345
Contact – Mr D Thompson

**Continental Illinois National
Bank & Trust Co of Chicago**
162 Queen Victoria Street
London EC4V 4BS
01-236 7444
Contact – Mr S Walker

Daiwa Bank Ltd
Condor House
14 St Paul's Churchyard
London EC4M 8BD
01-248 8080
Contact – Mr G Stevenson

**Dean Witter Capital Markets
International**
56 Leadenhall Street
London EC3A 2BH
01-480 8500
Contact – Miss S Patterson

Elders Securities UK Ltd
73 Cornhill
London EC3V 3QQ

01-283 7642
Contact — Mr J Pace

Exco Futures Ltd
105 Cannon Street
London EC4N 5AY
01-283 7642
Contact – Personnel Department

Robert Fleming Securities
25 Copthall Avenue
London EC2R 7DR
01-638 5858
Contact – Mr F Smith

The Fuji Bank Ltd
101 Moorgate
London EC2M 6TQ
01-638 1421
Contact Mr K Cripps

Gerrard & National Holdings plc
33 Lombard Street
London EC3V 9BQ
01-623 9981
Contact – Mr P Johnson

Gill & Duffus Ltd
St Dunstan's House
201 Borough High Street
London SE1 1HW
01-407 7050
Contact – Miss I Leek

GNI Ltd
Colchurch House
1 London Bridge Walk
London SE1 2SX
01-378 7171
Contact – Mr A Wilkinson

E F Hutton & Co (London)
Princess House
152–156 Upper Thames Street
London EC4R 3UH
021-623 0900/0800
Contact – Personnel Director

Kidder Peabody Securities
107 Cheapside
London EC2V 6DD

01-480 8200
Contact – Personnel Director

Merrill Lynch International
3 Newgate Street
London EC1A 7DA
01-382 8980
Contact – Mr K Robinson

Nomura International
24 Monument Street
London EC2R 8AJ
01-283 8811
Contact – Mr M Brookes

Paine Webber International
1 Finsbury Avenue
London EC2M 2PA
01-377 0055
Contact – Mr G Soper

Rudolf Wolff & Co
2nd Floor D Section
Plantation House
31–35 Fenchurch Street
London EC3M 3DX
01-626 8765
Contact – Mr P Ward

Saudi International Bank
99 Bishopsgate
London EC2M 2TB
01-638 2323
Contact – Personnel Department

Shearson Lehman Brothers International
9 Devonshire Square
London EC2M 4YL
01-626 2525
Contact – Personnel Department

For further details of financial futures brokers contact:

The London International Financial Futures Exchange
Royal Exchange
London EC3V 3PJ
01-623 0444

Fund Management Groups

Abbey Life Investment Services
80 Holdenhurst Road
Bournemouth
Hants BH8 8AL
0202 292373
Contact – Mr K Padderson

Allied Dunbar Unit Trusts plc
9–15 Sackville Street
Piccadilly
London W1X 1DE
01-434 3211
Contact – Mrs L Pearson

Arbuthnot Investment Management Services
131 Finsbury Pavement
Moorgate
London EC2A 1AY
01-628 9876
Contact – Mr L F Heasman

Baillie Gifford & Co
3 Glenfinlas Street
Edinburgh EH3 6YY
031-225 2581
Contact – Miss J McPherson

Barclays de Zoete Wedd Investment Management Ltd
Seal House
1 Swan Lane
London EC4R 3TH
01-623 7777
Contact – Personnel Department

Baring Investment Management Ltd
8 Bishopsgate
London EC2N 4AE
01-588 6133
Contact – Miss E Williams

British Coal Pension Scheme
Hobart House
Grosvenor Place
London SW1 7AE
01-235 2020

British Gas Corporation Pension Scheme
326 High Holborn
London WC1V 7PT

01-831 6272
Contact – Mr B L Edwards

British Steel Superannuation Scheme
9 Albert Embankment
London SE1 7SN
01-735 7654
Contact – Mr P E Oldham

Brown Shipley Asset Management Ltd
Eldon House
2–3 Eldon Street
London EC2M 7DU
01-377 1099
Contact – Personnel Department

Canada Life Unit Trust Managers Ltd
Canada Life House
High Street
Potters Bar
Herts EN6 5BA
0707 51122
Contact – Mrs C A Pritchard

James Capel & Co
James Capel House
PO Box 551
6 Bevis Marks
London EC3A 7JQ
01-621 0011
Contact – Personnel Department

Cater Allen Investment Management Ltd
1 King William Street
London EC4N 7AU
01-623 6314
Contact – Personnel Department

Charterhouse Investment Management Ltd
Capital House
2 Festival Square
Edinburgh EH 3 9SU
031-228 4477
Contact – Personnel Department

Clerical Medical Pension Fund Management Service
15 St James' Square
London SW1Y 4LQ

01-930 5474
Contact – Personnel Department

Commercial Union Investment Management
1 Undershaft
London EC3P 3DQ
01-283 7500
Contact – Personnel Department

County Investment Management Ltd
161 Cheapside
London EC2V 6EU
01-726 1633
Contact – Mr J Davey

Crown Unit Trust Services Ltd
Crown Life House
Woking
Surrey GU2 1XW
048 625033
Contact – Mr A Rudge

Dunedin Fund Managers Ltd
3 Charlotte Square
Edinburgh EH2 4DS
031-225 4571
Contact – Mr C Peters

Eagle Pension Funds Ltd
1 Threadneedle Street
London EC2R 8BE
01-588 1212
Contact – Mr T Allder

Edinburgh Fund Managers plc
4 Melville Crescent
Edinburgh EH3 7JB
031-226 4931
Contact — Mr M Bullick

Equity & Law Unit Trust Managers Ltd
20 Lincoln's Inn Fields
London WC2A 3ES
01-242 6844
Contact – Mr M Moss

Fidelity International Management Ltd
River Walk
Tonbridge

Kent TN9 1DY
0732 361144
Contact – Personnel Executive

**Robert Fleming Investment
Management Ltd**
25 Copthall Avenue
London EC2R 7DR
01-638 5858
Contact – Mr F Smith

**Foreign and Colonial
Management Ltd**
1 Laurence Pountney Hill
London EC4R 0BA
01-623 4680
Contact – Miss M Hum

**Framlington Investment
Management Ltd**
3 London Wall Buildings
London EC2M 5NQ
01-628 5151
Contact – Mrs P Durham

**Friend's Provident Unit Trust
Managers Ltd**
Pixham End
Dorking
Surrey RH 4 1QA
0306 885055
Contact – Personnel Department

**Gartmore Investment
Management Ltd**
2–4 St Mary Axe
London EC3A 8BP
01-623 1212
Contact – Mr R Jiggins

Globe Investment Trust plc
Electra House
Temple Place
London WC2R 3HP
01-836 7766
Contact – Mr P J Dyke

John Govett & Co Ltd
Winchester House
77 London Wall
London EC2N 1DH

01-588 5620
Contact – Personnel Department

Grofund Managers Ltd
Pinners Hall
8–9 Austin Friars
London EC2N 2AE
01-588 5317
Contact – Mr G Fraher

GT Management Ltd
8th Floor
8 Devonshire Square
London EC2M 4YJ
01-283 2575
Contact – Mr M Hill

Guardian Royal Exchange
Royal Exchange
London EC3V 3LS
01-283 7101
Contact – Mrs S Newman

**Guinness Mahon Fund Managers
Ltd**
PO Box 442
32 St Mary-at-Hill
London EC3P 3AJ
01–623 9333
Contact – Personnel Department

**Hambros Investment
Management Ltd**
41 Bishopsgate
London EC2P 2AA
01-588 2851
Contact – Personnel Department

**Henderson Pension Fund
Management Ltd**
26 Finsbury Square
London EC2A 1DA
01-638 5757
Contact – Mr C Day

**Hill Samuel Investment
Management Ltd**
45 Beech Street
London EC2P 2LX
01-628 8011
Contact – Mr J Miller

Ivory & Sime plc
One Charlotte Square
Edinburgh EH2 4DZ
031-225 1357
Contact – Mr J Hayward

Kleinwort Grieveson Investment Management Ltd
20 Fenchurch Street
London EC3P 3DB
01-623 8000
Contact – Personnel Department

Lazard Securities Ltd
21 Moorfields
London EC2P 2HT
01-588 2721
Contact – Mr G McFeely

Legal and General Investment Management Ltd
Bucklersbury House
Temple Court
11 Queen Victoria Street
London EC4N 4TP
01-248 9678
Contact – Mr J MacCarthy

Lloyds Bank Fund Management Ltd
Elizabeth House
9–11 Bush Lane
London EC4P 4LN
01-623 1288
Contact – Personnel Department

M & G Investment Management Ltd
Three Quays
Tower Hill
London EC3R 6BQ
01-626 4588
Contact – L E Linaker

Manulife Management Ltd
Manulife House
St George's Way
Stevenage
Herts SG1 1HP

0438 356101
Contact – Mr M Austin

Martin Currie Investment Management
29 Charlotte Square
Edinburgh EH2 4HA
031-225 3811
Contact – Mr D C Skinner

Mercury Warburg Investment Management Ltd
33 King William Street
London EC4R 9AS
01-280 2800
Contact – Personnel Department

Midland Bank Investment Department
47 Cannon Street
London EC4M 5SQ
01-606 9911
Contact – Personnel Department

Mim Ltd
11 Devonshire Square
London EC2M 4YR
01-626 3434
Contact – Mr R J Duthie

Morgan Grenfell Investment Management Ltd
46 New Broad Street
London EC2M 1NB
01-256 7500
Contact – Mr P Lefevre

Murray Johnstone Ltd
163 Hope Street
Glasgow G2 2UH
041-221 5521
Contact – Mrs S Lamont

National Provident Investment Managers Ltd
PO Box 227
48 Gracechurch Street
London EC3P 3HH
01-623 4200
Contact – Personnel Department

**Oppenheimer Fund
Management Ltd**
Mercantile House
66 Cannon Street
London EC4N 6AE
01-236 1425
Contact – Mrs C Shaw

Pearl Trust Managers Ltd
252 High Holborn
London WC1V 7EB
01-405 8441
Contact — Group Administrator
Recruitment and Training

**Phillips and Drew Fund
Management Ltd**
120 Moorgate
London EC2M 6XP
01-628 4444
Contact – Mrs S Mew

**PosTel Investment
Management Ltd**
Equitable House
48 King William Street
London EC4R 9DD
01-626 4577
Contact – Personnel Department

**Prudential Portfolio
Managers Ltd**
142 Holborn Bars
London EC1N 2NH
01-405 9222
Contact – Mr G Keeys

**N M Rothschild Asset
Management Ltd**
New Court
St Swithin's Lane
London EC4P 4DU
01-280 5000
Contact – Mr A May

**Royal Trust Company of
Canada, The**
Royal Trust House
48–50 Cannon Street
London EC4N 6LD

01-236 6044
Contact – Personnel Department

Save & Prosper Group Ltd
1 Finsbury Avenue
London EC2M 2QY
01-588 1717
Contact – Mr K Nicholson

**Schroder Investment
Management Ltd**
36 Old Jewry
London EC2R 8BS
01-382 6000
Contact – Personnel Department

**Scottish Amicable Investment
Managers Ltd**
150 St Vincent Street
Glasgow G2 5NQ
041 248 2323
Contact – Personnel Department

**Scottish Widows Fund
Management Ltd**
15 Dalkeith Road
Edinburgh EH16 5BU
031-665 6000
Contact – Mr A Macintyre

Singer & Friedlander Ltd
21 New Street
Bishopsgate
London EC2M 4HR
01-623 3000
Contact – Mr B Eldred

Stewart Ivory & Co Ltd
45 Charlotte Square
Edinburgh EH2 4HW
031-26 3271
Contact – Mr W Walker

**Thornton Investment
Management Ltd**
Park House
16 Finsbury Circus
London EC2M 7DJ
01-638 4766
Contact – Miss C Richards

Touche Remnant & Co
Mermaid House
2 Puddle Dock
London EC4V 3AT
01-236 6565
Contact – Mr N Fitzgerald

Wood Mackenzie & Co Ltd
100 Wood Street
London EC2P 2AJ
01-600 3600
Contact – Mr D Boath

Merchant Banks

Henry Ansbacher
Priory House
1 Mitre Square
London EC3A 5AN
01-283 2500
Contact – Mrs P Clark

ANZ Merchant Bank
65 Holborn Viaduct
London EC1A 2EU
01-489 0021
Contact – Personnel Department

Arbuthnot Latham Bank
131 Finsbury Pavement
Moorgate
London EC2A 1AY
01-280 8400
Contact – Personnel Department

Baring Brothers
8 Bishopsgate
London EC2N 4AE
01-283 8833
Contact – Miss E Williams

The British Linen Bank
4 Melville Street
Edinburgh EH3 7NZ
031-226 4071
Contact – Mr P Cockburn

Brown Shipley
Founders Court
Lothbury
London EC2R 7HE
01-606 9833
Contact – Personnel Department

James Capel Bankers Ltd
7 Devonshire Square
London EC2M 4HN
01-626 0566
Contact – Personnel Department

Charterhouse Bank
1 Paternoster Row
St Paul's
London EC4M 7DH
01-248 4000
Contact – Mr J McCarthy

Citicorp
335 Strand
London WC2R 1LS
01-836 1230
Contact – Ms S Day

County Ltd
Drapers Gardens
12 Throgmorton Avenue
London EC2P 2ES
01-638 6000
Contact – Personnel Department

First Boston Corporation
22 Bishopsgate
London EC2N 4BQ
01-283 3188
Contact – Miss S Pearce

Robert Fleming
25 Copthall Avenue
London EC2R 7DR
01-638 5858
Contact – Mr F Smith

Gresham Trust
Barrington House
Gresham Street
London EC2V 7HE
01-606 6474
Contact – Mr K Croswell

Guinness Mahon & Co Ltd
32 St Mary-at-Hill
London EC3P 3AJ
01-623 9333
Contact – Personnel Department

Hambros Bank
41 Bishopsgate
London EC2P 2AA
01-588 2851
Contact – Personnel Department

Henderson Administration Ltd
26 Finsbury Square
London EC2 1DA
01-638 5757
Contact – Mr C W Clifford

Hill Samuel
100 Wood Street
London EC2P 2AJ
01-628 8011
Contact – Mr R Gardener

Industrial Finance & Investment Cprn plc
Well Court House
8–9 Well Court
London EC4M 9DN
01-726 4841
Contact – Mr C C Norland

Kleinwort Benson Ltd
20 Fenchurch Street
London EC3P 3DB
01-623 8000
Contact – Personnel Department

Lazard Brothers
21 Moorfields
London EC2P 2HT
01-588 2721
Contact – Mr G McFeely

Lloyds Merchant Bank
PO Box 241
40–66 Queen Victoria Street
London EC4P 4EL
01-248 2244
Contact – Personnel Department

Manufacturers Hanover Trust
7 Princes Street
London EC2P 2AX
01-600 5666
Contact – Mr M Frost

Minster Trust
Minster House
Arthur Street
London EC4R 9BH
01-623 1050
Contact – Mr D F Loader

Samuel Montagu
10 Lower Thames Street
London EC2R 6AE
Contact – Mr J Young

Morgan Grenfell Group
23 Great Winchester Street
London EC2P 2AX
01-588 4545
Contact – Mr P Lefevre

Morgan Guaranty Trust Company of New York
Morgan House
Angel Court
London EC2R 7AE
01-600 2300
Contact – Personnel Department

Rea Brothers
Aldermans House
Aldermans Walk
London EC2M 3XR
01-623 1155
Contact – Miss H Schulze

NM Rothschild & Sons
PO Box 185
New Court
St Swithin's Lane
London EC4P 4DU
01-280 5000
Contact – Mr D Sullivan

Saudi International Bank
99 Bishopsgate
London EC2M 2TB
01-638 2323
Contact – Personnel Department

J Henry Schroder Wagg & Co
120 Cheapside
London EC2V 6DS
01-382 6000
Contact – Miss S Cox

Singer & Friedlander
21 New Street
Bishopsgate
London EC2M 4HR
Contact – Mr B Eldred

Standard Chartered Merchant Bank
33–36 Gracechurch Street
London EC3V 0AX
01-623 8711
Contact – Mrs J Phillip

SG Warburg
33 King William Street
London EC4R 9AS
01-280 2222
Contact – Personnel Department

Commercial/Clearing Banks

Bank of Scotland
Staff Training Centre
58–62 St Alban's Road
Edinburgh EH9 2LX
031-442 7777
Contact – Mr J S Henderson
(Assistant General Manager)

Barclays Bank
Fleetway House
25 Farringdon Street
London EC4A 5LP
01-248 1234
Contact – Mr R W Ellis
(Manager – Graduate Recruitment)

Lloyds Bank plc
Black Horse House
78 Cannon Street
London EC4P 4LN
01-236 9332
Contact – Mr P McNamara
(Manager, Graduate Recruitment)

Midland Bank
Recruitment and Development Office
1st Floor
Buchanan House
London EC1N 2HY
01-260 8000
Contact – Mr J Bosworth

National Westminster Bank
Recruitment Department
National House
14 Moorgate
London EC2R 6BS

01-726 1674
Contact – Graduate Appointments
Officer

Royal Bank of Scotland
42 St Andrew Square
Edinburgh EH2 2YE
031-556 8555
Contact – Mr A Ross

Standard Chartered Bank
38 Bishopsgate
London EC2N 4DE
01-280 7500
Contact – Graduate Recruitment
and Development Officer

TSB Group
Head Office
PO Box 33
25 Milk Street
London EC2V 8LU
01-606 7070
Contact – Graduate Recruitment
Officer

Accountancy Firms

Armitage & Norton
28 Southampton Buildings
Chancery Lane
London WC2A 1AR
01-242 1937
Contact – Mrs A Mitchell

Arthur Andersen & Co
1 Surrey Street
London WC2R 2PS
01-836 1200
Contact – Mr P Russell

Arthur Young
7 Rolls Buildings
Fetter Lane
London EC4A 1NH
01-831 7130
Contact – Ms M Eastwood

Baker Rooke
99 Aldwych
London WC2B 4JY
01-242 0211
Contact – Miss S D Henry

Ball Baker Leake
36 Essex Street

London WC2R 3AS
01-583 1188
Contact – Mr J Collard

Barron Rowles & Bass
12 John Street
London WC1N 2EB
01-242 5891
Contact – Training Partner

Binder Hamlyn BDO
1 Sergeants Inn
London EC4Y 1JD
01-353 2000
Contact – Ms S Burke

Bowker Orford
15–19 Cavendish Place
London W1M ODD
01-636 6391
Contact — Mr A Kay

Brebner Allen & Trapp
109 Baker Street
London W1M 2BH
01-486 0188
Contact – Mrs J Davies

Bright Grahame Murray & Co
124–130 Seymour Place
London W1H 6AA
01-402 5201
Contact – Mr H Bernstein

Buzzacott
8 Salisbury Square
London EC4Y 8HR
01-353 8022
Contact – Mr A Simpson

Chantrey Wood King
1 Old Burlington Street
London W1X 2AX
01-437 0633
Contact – Miss C Knapp

Clark Whitehill
25 New Street Square
London EC4A 3LN
01-353 1577
Contact – Training Department

Comins & Co
22 St Andrew Street
London EC4A 3AN
01-353 5691
Contact – Mr M Simon

Cooper Lancaster
Aldwych House
71–91 Aldwych
London WC2B 4HN
01-242 2444
Contact – Training Department

Coopers & Lybrand
Plumtree Court
London EC4A 4HT
01-583 500
Contact – Mr D Weeks

Deloitte Haskins & Sells
PO Box 207
128 Queen Victoria Street
London EC4P 4JX
01-248 3913
Contact – Mr I du Pre

Dixon Wilson
Gillett House
55 Basinghall Street
London EC2V 5EA
01-628 4321
Contact – Mrs C Brookes

Ernst & Whinney
Becket House
1 Lambeth Palace Road
London SE1 7EU
01-928 2000
Contact – Mrs I Pattison

Finnie & Co
Kreston House
8 Gate Street
London WC2A 3HJ
01-831 9100
Contact – Mr M J Robinson

H W Fisher & Co
69–76 Long Acre
London WC2E 9JW
01-379 3461
Contact — Mr S Lesser

Fox & Hoare
6 Wardrobe Place
Carter Lane
London EC4V 5HR

01-248 4767
Contact – Training Department

Grant Thornton
Fairfax House
Fulwood Place
London WC1V 6DW
01-405 8422
Contact – Mrs A Tovell

Hacker Young
2 Fore Street
London EC2Y 5DH
01-588 3611
Contact – Mr P M Hollins

Hays Allan
17 High Holborn
London WC1V 7NL
01-831 6233
Contact – Training Department

Hereward Scott Davies & Co
Hillside House
2–6 Friern Park
London N12 9BY
01-446 4371
Contact – Training Partner

Hodgson Impey
6 Long Lane
London EC1A 9DP
01-606 6441
Contact – Training Manager

Hope Agar
Epworth House
25–35 City Road
London EC1Y 1AR
01-628 5801
Contact – Training Partner

Howard Tilly
Commonwealth House
1 New Oxford Street
London WC1A 1PF
01-404 5541
Contact – Training Manager

Hughes Allen
Greenwood House

4–7 Salisbury Court
London EC4Y 8BT
01-583 7575
Contact – Mr D Thomas

Hugill & Co
38 Chancery Lane
London WC2A 1EL
01-242 4674/5318
Contact – Mrs N Thornton

Jeffreys Henry Rudolf & Marks
Wilec House
82–84 City Road
London EC1Y 2DA
01-253 7064
Contact – Training Manager

Kidsons
Columbia House
69 Aldwych
London WC2B 4DY
01-405 9292/0616
Contact – Staff Partner

Kingsford's
23 Essex Street
Strand
London WC2R 3AW
01-836 4773/4560
Contact – Mr T Hanson

Lubbock Fine
3–5 Bedford Row
London WC1R 4DB
01-242 9881
Contact – Personnel Officer

MacIntyre Hudson
28 Ely Place
London EC1N 6RL
01-242 0242
Contact – Mr H Bell-Roberts

Milne Ross
Chapel House
12a Upper Berkeley Street
London W1H 7PE
01-262 7788
Contact – Mr R Casling

Moore Stephens
St Paul's House
Warwick Lane
London EC4P 4BN
01-248 4499
Contact – Miss V Burch

Moores & Rowland
Cliffords Inn
Fetter Lane
London EC4A 1AS
01-831 2345
Contact – Training Department

Morgan Brown & Haynes
89 Fleet Street
London EC4Y 1EB
01-353 3895
Contact – Miss F Probert

Morison Stoneham
805 Salisbury House
31 Finsbury Circus
London EC2M 5SQ
01-628 2040
Contact – Mr M Bailey

Morley & Scott
Lynton House
7–12 Tavistock Square
London WC1H 9LT
01-387 5868
Contact – Mr R Jones

Neville Russell
246 Bishopsgate
London EC2M 4PB
01-377 1000
Contact – Mr S Rochester

Pannell Kerr Forster
New Garden House
78 Hatton Garden
London EC1N 8JA
01-831 7393
Contact – Mr P Strode

Peat Marwick McLintock
1 Puddle Dock
Blackfriars
London EC4V 3PD

01-236 8000
Contact — Mr A Kingsley

Price Waterhouse
Southwark Towers
32 London Bridge Street
London SE1 9SY
01-407 8989
Contact – Mr M Jennings

Pridie Brewster
Carolyn House
29–31 Greville Street
London EC1N 8RB
01-831 8821
Contact – Training Manager

Reads & Co
Leith House
47 Gresham Street
London EC2V 7ET
01-606 3080
Contact – Training Partner

Robson Rhodes
186 City Road
London EC1V 2NU
01-251 1644
Contact – Personnel Department

Russell Limebeer
Pembroke House
40 City Road
London EC1Y 2AD
01-251 2681
Contact – Mr C Hunt

Saffery Champness
St Martin's House
16 St Martin's-le-Grand
London EC1A 4EP
01-600 0818
Contact – Mr D S Watson

Silver Altman
High Holborn House
52–54 High Holborn
London WC1V 6RT
01-405 9421
Contact – Mr R Evans

Smallfield Rawlins
Beadle House
47–49 Borough High Street
London SE1 1NJ
01-403 5900
Contact – Training Manager

Spicer and Pegler
Friary Court
65 Crutched Friars
London EC3N 2NP
01-480 7766
Contact – Mrs A Robinson,
Human Resources

Stoy Hayward
8 Baker Street
London W1M 1DA
01-486 5888
Contact – Miss K Rundle

Touche Ross
Hill House
1 Little New Street
London EC4A 3TR
01-353 8011
Contact – Mrs D Sansom

Wilkins Kennedy
Bridge House
London Bridge
London SE1 9QR
01-403 1877
Contact – Training Manager

Tax Work

Arthur Andersen & Co
1 Surrey Street
London WC2R 2PS
01-836 1200
Contact — Mr P Russell

Arthur Young
7 Rolls Buildings
Fetter Lane
London EC4A 1NH
01-831 7130
Contact – Ms M Eastwood

Barron Rowles & Bass
12 John Street

London WC1N 2EB
01-242 5891
Contact – Training Partner

**The Civil Service Commission
(Tax Inspectorate)**
Alencon Link
Basingstoke
Hampshire RG21 1JB
0256 468551

Coopers & Lybrand
Plumtree Court
London EC4A 4HT
01-583 5000
Contact – Personnel Department

Deloitte Haskins & Sells
PO Box 207
128 Queen Victoria Street
London EC4P 4JX
01-248 3913
Contact – Mr I du Pre

Ernst & Whinney
Becket House
1 Lambeth Palace Road
London SE1 7EU
01-928 2000
Contact – Mrs I Pattison

Grant Thornton
Fairfax House
Fulwood Place
London WC1V 6DW
01-405 8422
Contact – Mrs A Tovell

Hodgson Impey
6 Long Lane
London EC1A 9DP
01-606 6441
Contact – Training Manager

Neville Russell
246 Bishopsgate
London EC2M 4PB
01-377 1000
Contact – Mr S Rochester

Peat Marwick McLintock
1 Puddle Dock
Blackfriars
London EC4V 3PD
01-236 8000
Contact – Personnel Department

Price Waterhouse
Southwark Towers
32 London Bridge Street
London SE1 9SY
01-407 8989
Contact – Personnel Department

Spicer and Pegler
Friary Court
65 Crutched Friars
London EC3N 2NP
01-480 7766
Contact – Mrs A Robinson,
Human Resources

Touche Ross & Co
Hill House
1 Little New Street
London EC4A 3TR
01-353 8011
Contact – Mrs D Sansom

Management Consultancy Firms

Arthur Andersen & Co
Management Consultants
1 Surrey Street
London WC2R 2PS
01-836 1200
Contact – Ms L Hopkins

Arthur Young
7 Rolls Buildings
Fetter Lane
London EC4A 1NH
01-831 7130
Contact – Ms M Eastwood

Bain & Co
6 Connaught Place
London W2 2ES
1-723 0208
Contact AC Recruiting Co-ordinator

Coopers & Lybrand
Plumtree Court
London EC4A 4HT
1-583 5000
Contact – Personnel Manager

Deloitte Haskins & Sells
PO Box 207
28 Queen Victoria Street
London EC4P 4JX

01-248 3913
Contact – Personnel Department

Ernst & Whinney
Becket House
1 Lambeth Palace Road
London SE1 7EU
01-928 2000
Contact – Mrs I Pattison

Hay-MSL Management Consultants Group
52 Grosvenor Gardens
London SW1W OAW
01-730 0833
Contact – Ms J Blakeley

Inbucon Management Consultants Ltd
Knightsbridge House
197 Knightsbridge
London SW7 1RN
01-584 6171
Contact – Mr P Moriss

McKinsey & Co
74 St James's Street
London SW1A 1PS
01-839 8040/2221
Contact – Mr A Turner

PA Management Consultants
Bowater House East
68 Knightsbridge
London SW1X 7LJ
01-589 7050
Contact – Mr G Syrett

P-E International
Park House
Wick Road
Egham
Surrey TW20 0HW
0784 34411
Contact – Personnel Department

Peat Marwick McLintock
1 Puddle Dock
Blackfriars
London EC4V 3PD
01-236 8000
Contact – Personnel Department

Financial Public Relations

Charles Barker City Ltd
30 Farringdon Street
London EC4A 4EA
01-634 1000
Contact – Mrs M Coles

Binns Cornwall and Partners
36 St Andrew's Hill
London EC4V 5DE
01-489 1441
Contact — Mr P Binns

Broad Street Group
30 Furnival Street
London WC1A 2PX
01-831 3113
Contact — Mrs G Pimm

Burson-Marsteller Financial
24–28 Bloomsbury Way
London WC1A 2PX
01-405 0937
Contact – Mrs S Knight

**City and Commercial
Communications Ltd**
Bell Court House
11 Blomfield Street
London EC2M 7AY
01-588 6050
Contact – Miss A Bell

Dewe Rogerson Ltd
London Wall Buildings
London Wall
London EC2M 5SY
01-638 9571
Contact – Mr B Kirkham

**Grandfield Rork Collins
Financial Ltd**
Prestige House
14–18 Holborn
London EC1N 2LE
01-242 2002
Contact – Mr A Watson

Hill Murray & Co
Giltspur House
Giltspur Street
London EC1A 9DE
01-489 0899
Contact – Mr R Hill

Walter Judd Ltd
1a Bow Lane
London EC4M 9EJ
01-236 4541
Contact – Mr R Springgay

Kingsway Public Relations
10 Doughty Street
London WC1N 2PL
01-831 6131
Contact – Miss B Jakens

Lombard Communications Ltd
127 Cheapside
London EC2V 6BT
01-600 0064
Contact – Miss F Scholes

Lowe-Bell Financial Ltd
1 Red Lion Court
London EC4A SEB
01-353 9203
Contact – Mrs K Trombley

McCann Consultancy
Hazlitt House
4 Bouverie Street
London EC4Y 8AB
01-353 5272
Contact – Mrs K Dunbar

Shandwick Consultants Ltd
Dauntsey House
Frederick's Place
Old Jewry
London EC2R 8AB
01-606 0680
Contact – Mrs R Weir

**St James's Corporate
Communications Ltd**
St James's House
4–7 Red Lion Court
London EC4A 3EB
01-583 2525
Contact – Mr M Arundell

Streets Financial Strategy
1 Bolt Court
London EC4A 3DQ
01-583 1544
Contact – Mrs A Sharp

Valin Pollen Ltd
46 Grosvenor Gardens
London SW1W 0EB

01-730 3456
Contact – Miss P Rome

Financial Publications

Accountancy
40 Bernard Street
London WC1N 1LD
01-628 7060
Editor – Mr G Holmes

Accountancy Age
VNU Publications
32–34 Broadwick Street
London W1A 2HG
01-439 4242
Editor – Mr R Bruce

The Banker
102–108 Clerkenwell Road
London EC1M 5SA
01-251 9321
Editor – Mr G Schreeve

Certified Accountant
Chapter Three Publications
Dartford
Kent DA1 1BX
0322 28584
Editor – Mr R Garlick

Euromoney
Euromoney Publications plc
Nestor House

Playhouse Yard
London EC4V 5EX
01-236 3288
Editor – Mr N Osborn

Financial Times Business Publishing Ltd
Greystoke Place
Fetter Lane
London EC4A 1MD
01-405 6969
Editor – Mrs G O'Connor
  (*Investors Chronicle*)
Editor – Mrs J Walford
  (*Money Management*)
Editor – Mrs K Jones
  (*Pensions Management*)

United Trade Press
UTP House
33–35 Bowling Green Lane
London EC1R 0DA
01-837 1212
Editor – Ms J Finch (*Insurance Age*)
Editor – Ms S Grandison
  (*Pensions Magazine*)
Editor – Ms L Walkington
  (*Planned Savings*)

Prepare Yourself to Get the Job

Before you go looking for the particular job that interests you it's important to find out as much as possible about the companies you want to work for, to present a good curriculum vitae, and to conduct yourself well at the interview stage. This brief guide to negotiating these various hurdles isn't meant to be gospel but simply an indication of how to improve your chances. By thinking about the points and issues raised you should stand that important step closer to securing a career in the City.

Do Your Homework

Before you start applying for the jobs which you think will suit you it is essential to do your homework. First try to find out as much as possible about the different careers on offer. By reading this book you should have gained at least some inkling of the sort of career that will appeal to you. If not, all well and good; at least you have saved yourself a lot of time! It is vitally important to be honest with yourself at this stage. If you don't like selling then don't go for a sales job, however well paid and glamorous it might seem. If you don't like getting up in the morning you're also going to have to think twice. Nowadays it is not at all uncommon to see people starting work in the City at 7.30 am.

When you have targeted specific areas which look interesting you should go to your careers office to try to gain more information. Talk to your careers officer; he might be able to help you out or put you in touch with someone in the particular business. If you know someone in the business that's even better: try to arrange a visit to their workplace so you can get a better idea of what the job entails. If nothing else you'll be able to ask questions about the important changes which are taking place in the industry/profession, the most highly regarded companies or firms in the business, and the day-to-day routine of the job, all of which will come in very useful when you actually go for a job interview. Armed with this information you will at least be able to demonstrate some in-depth knowledge of current developments in the business and, by finding out about the types of people who work in the business you should be in a better position to demonstrate to your interviewer just why he should employ you in preference to anyone else.

Depending on the job you are going for it might be worth getting to grips with the *Financial Times*. This isn't an absolute prerequisite but it should enable you to keep abreast of developments in the City. What's more, it's the sort of discipline which you will have to get into at some stage anyway.

CVs and Covering Letters

Once you have decided on the career you want to pursue you will need to devote a fair amount of time to compiling a CV and a good covering letter with which to approach prospective employers. Persistence will pay off here. Apply to as many companies and firms as possible. If it seems a bit of a bind or not worth your while, then perhaps you should be thinking of working elsewhere. Most City careers are very demanding with long hours and constant pressure. If you baulk at the thought of photocopying and posting 100 CVs then perhaps you're not cut out for it. Expense is another thing which shouldn't get in your way: £100 on photocopying, phone calls, stamps etc might seem like a lot of money now but in three years' time when you're earning upwards of £30,000, it could well prove to be the most profitable investment you ever made!

When you send a CV you should also send a covering letter which explains why you are writing to the company in question, ie which area of the business you want to work in, and things you have done which are relevant for the job. For example you might have graduated in an arts discipline but it could be that you also did accountancy or economics as a subsidiary subject. Try not to make judgements about yourself: 'I am a self starter'. It's much better to point to what you have done and leave others to work out what it means: 'During the summer holidays I worked for two months at an accountancy firm in my local town'.

Both the covering letter and the CV are vitall

important. Most jobs in the City involve a degree of selling in one way or another. Financial products rely heavily of personalities to sell them because, in many instances, it is virtually impossible to differentiate one product from another (a bit like petrol!). So one of the vital factors in the selling process is the individual who is representing the company. Your covering letter and CV are serving a similar purpose: they are your initial sales pitch to your prospective employer. If they are not properly thought out, or badly presented, he can draw only one conclusion — that you are not particularly keen and probably won't be very good at your job! One of the major mistakes is to make covering letters far too long. This should be avoided at all costs. The person reading them will probably have received so many applications that he or she will only be able to glance very quickly at each one.

You should also try to personalise your covering letter. Nowadays more people have access to word processors and will tend to do their CVs on them. That's fine, because it shows you have some proficiency with modern technology and that you're not scared of using it. However, if you are going to use a standard word-processed letter try to find out the name of the recruitment officer at the firm to which you are writing so that you can personalise the letter. Otherwise he might think that you have done little more than photocopy the letter, which indicates that you don't have a particular interest in his firm.

On the CV you should list your academic achievements (O levels, A levels, degree etc) and any other achievements which are important to you or which you think are particularly relevant. In this category you should put things like sports, clubs or political affiliations. Anything which involves teamwork is especially important for a number of reasons.

First, in most financial jobs, especially those in the City, there will be a good deal of teamwork. It is absolutely essential that you are able to communicate and mix effectively with the other members of the team or else you won't operate satisfactorily. Social activities also demonstrate an ability to get on well with other people. Again, we come back to the selling side of the City. Most of the jobs, especially the ones which graduates go for, will be high profile. You will be dealing with people from outside the firm, either face-to-face or over the telephone. Obviously, as you progress the importance of this role will increase to the point where you could be the only contact or at least the initial contact which a client has with your firm. Therefore, it is crucial that you can get on well with your fellows. In many respects this helps to explain why, for many years, the City had such a cliquish air about it. Most of the people employed there had similar backgrounds, were members of the same clubs, and could get on very well with one another. But it was difficult for outsiders to break in because they hadn't been to the 'right' schools or universities and they weren't members of the 'right' clubs. All this is, of course, rapidly changing, but it is still very important to be able to mix socially.

An ability to mix and operate in a team equally comes into play if you want to move up by the management route. In many of the careers presently on offer in the City work pressure is such that early responsibility is the norm rather than the exception. This will usually entail running a department with a number of other people in it and management and people skills are of paramount importance in this situation. Again, time pressures mean that management training in some cases will leave a lot to be desired so the employer will be looking for people who can take on the responsibilities with the absolute minimum of fuss.

One useful extra tip for your covering letter/CV is to try and use active verbs wherever appropriate, such as: initiate, formulate, launch, construct, negotiate, organise, co-ordinate, plan and develop. They all give the impression that you are proactive: instead of just having a situation thrust upon you, you are the sort of person who can take control of the situation and make it work in your favour. This should help to liven up the letter/CV a little and will probably appeal to American employers.

Getting the Interview

Once you have decided who you want to apply to and have constructed your CV and covering letter, you are ready to move. One important and useful trick is to apply to companies that you don't really want to work for as well as for ones that you do. Try to pick companies in the same field of business. The object of this exercise is to get some experience of interviewing behind you before you actually go for the big one. After all, if you go for a job that you really want without any interview experience your chances must be severely diminished.

Find out if any companies in the field of business in which you are interested are visiting your university or run seminars at their offices. If so, try to go along. That way you can probably get a head start by finding out a little bit more about the job, but more importantly, if you buttonhole the right person – especially after a few drinks – you can find out what sort of person they are looking for and the sort of questions they like to be asked at interviews. This technique can definitely work and should in no way be underestimated!

Once you have posted off your application you may think that it is all in the lap of the gods. Not so. There are several things you can do to maximise your chance of getting that all-important interview. To some people, the following techniques may seem a little trite or not quite the sort of thing which they'd be caught doing. Fine, if you know that you will definitely get the job you want in finance. If your mind doesn't work that way and you are a little frightened of being too brash then perhaps you should reconsider working in finance. Some of the jobs available are extremely tough going, involving very long hours and extreme dedication (at the same time they also pay good money). In short, they deserve to be taken very seriously. There is only a limited number of jobs available so you need to try very hard to get that interview.

Here are several techniques which you might like to try. The first is to phone up the company to find out the name of the person in charge of recruiting for the particular job that you want. At least that way you can personalise the letter. Next best is to talk to them, explain your position and see if they're interested in you. If they are they will ask you to send your CV and, with a bit of luck, you should stick in their minds. At least that way when your CV arrives it will be given close consideration. Best of all is to talk to the head of department for which you want to work. To do this you are going to need a lot of confidence and you will have to do your background work to ensure that at least you have some idea of what you are talking about. If you use this method bear in mind that these people are always very busy. However, this works in your favour because it means that they will invariably work late so you can phone them after 6.00 pm (ie cheap rate) and the hubbub in the office will probably have died down so they will have time to talk. Having said that you should keep your conversation as brief as possible. Simply explain your position and see what the reaction is. Admittedly, to do this takes quite a lot of nerve and most people are happier just writing a letter. That's all well and good, but remember that the types of job available in the City will usually require a good deal of telephone work and will involve talking to people you have never met before, trying either to get information out of them or to sell them something. If you're not happy doing this then think what it will be like doing it day in and day out for a living!

Another technique is to follow up your application. Nowadays workloads have become so heavy that some companies can't even be bothered to write a rejection letter to unsuccessful applicants. This rather unhelpful practice means that it is always a good idea to keep track of your applications, if only to set your mind at ease as to whether you have been selected or not. However, the primary reason for doing it is to try to push your application gently through all the red tape. It could simply be that your letter has landed on someone's desk and they just haven't had time to look at it. By phoning up after about two to three weeks you should get some action if only through the guilt factor! It is true to say that if you go too far with these techniques prospective employers could take a very negative and possibly a derogatory view. Fine. Let them do that. Just ask yourself how long they are going to last in an international environment with competition which is both very brash and very powerful. No one knows the answer, of course, but we can all hazard a guess!

Coping With the Interview

The next hurdle you have to confront is the dreaded interview. All sorts of things can happen at this stage most of which you will have no control over. For example, if your interviewer is having a bad day or doesn't like the colour of your shoes then you might not get in! On the other hand, he might be having a good day. So in the end it's all swings and roundabouts. Apart from the ordeal of actually being interviewed you might also have to do a psychological test. Again, you have no control over this as you won't know exactly what answers they are looking for. In these circumstances there is nothing you can do to alter the outcome so you must simply rely on the accuracy of the test. Another point to remember is that during the interview you should try to act as much like yourself as possible. After all, if you have to lie about yourself to get a particular job the chances are that you won't enjoy it.

Make the Ordeal as Pleasant as Possible
So what can you do to ensure that your interview is a pleasant experience? Do your background research. Get hold of a copy of

the latest annual report of the company (if appropriate). Go to the careers office and find out as much as you can about the company and keep an eye on the newspapers for any interesting snippets of news or gossip which you could bring up during the interview.

The next thing you should do is to try to take control of the interview. By doing so you are putting yourself in a much better position. Remember that the person who is interviewing you might just be as nervous as you are and in many instances will not be a professional interviewer. He will probably be pleasantly relieved if you take over the reins at times and let him take a more passive role.

It is absolutely impossible to know how an interview will go before you get in there. Nevertheless you must do your background reading so that you are prepared for the sorts of question that might come flying at you. Typical examples are, 'Why are you interested in this firm?', 'Why are you interested in this job?' through to the more high pressure questions such as, 'Are you decisive?' and 'Why should we take you on at this firm?'

If you prepare properly you should be able to field these questions fairly easily. Bear in mind that your interviewers don't expect you to have in-depth knowledge of their business; they are more interested in how you react to various questions. For example, a story which is apocryphal but demonstrates the point fairly well is of an undergraduate who went for an interview at a merchant bank and was asked to tell the interviewer about the Portuguese economy. The undergraduate knew nothing but still managed to talk for half an hour and got the job. Why? Because he wasn't asked to tell the interviewer what he *knew* about the Portuguese economy but simply to tell him about it. This is important because in your day-to-day job you might often get asked questions to which you don't know the answer. So long as you are careful it is still possible to give a reply which implies you know what you are talking about and you can always check the facts later.

Be Positive and Enthusiastic

It is extremely important to sell yourself. Dwell on the positive, be enthusiastic. There is nothing worse for an employer than sitting in a room with an interviewee who sounds as though he is bored senseless. It is off-putting, embarrassing and, worse still, the employers know that they are wasting their time and yours because they can't possibly employ someone like you in a position where you might have to meet their clients.

Again, it's down to the selling aspect. It is vitally important to turn on the charm. If you can't then perhaps you should reconsider your desire to work in the square mile.

Stress Interviews

At some stage you might be faced with what is euphemistically described as a 'stress' interview. Here the interviewer is apparently trying to find out how the 'victim' will react under stress. Such interviews are invariably very embarrassing, not least because the interviewer usually shows himself up to be a prize wally. It might occur to you that in a real life situation the most obstreperous client could not possibly be so rude, which leads to the conclusion that you are being 'prepared' for the sort of office atmosphere you can expect when you start work. If that's the case then you should ask yourself whether you think it is really worth while going to work there.

Pressure interviews will vary from organisation to organisation. Sometimes the interview will be conducted by just one person in which case he will probably be a little bit embarrassed at using the technique and you can use this embarrassment to get the upper hand. In other situations you will have two or three people firing questions at you in quick succession. Stress interviews usually involve the technique of asking ridiculous questions such as 'Are you decisive?'. No doubt most people could talk for ages on what constitutes a decision before they ever got to the question of whether they ever made one!

Again, it is almost impossible to learn how to react in a stress interview so you might as well just take it in your stride as and when it comes. One technique which is said to be useful is to imagine the interviewer in a silly situation like sitting on a toilet. This brings him down to an absurd level and should boost your confidence.

Silence

Most people find silences or pauses in conversations very embarrassing. It usually stops the flow and if you allow it to take control you will soon lose the gist of the conversation and you will not be able to move on with a sensible question. One way of getting around this is to carry a small note pad – nothing too obtrusive – with a list of question in it. If you get stuck, simply refer to your notebook. Do not be too embarrassed to use this technique. Your interviewer will probably understand that you are quite nervous. He should also realise that, although you have done your background research, you will not necessarily know a huge amount about his business. So you will need a notebook to remind you of the various areas you want to discuss.

Always bear in mind that an interview is not some sort of examination where you are expected to remember everything. In fact, there are two reasons why having a notebook will look more impressive than not having one. First, it shows that you have taken the time to study the company so that you can actually ask some intelligent questions. The fact that you have bothered to write these all down indicates that you are thorough and expect answers to all your questions – not just the ones that you have managed to memorise. Second, it shows a professional approach. After all, in a business meeting it is more likely than not that you will be taking notes instead of working from memory. As this interview is a very important point in your life, why shouldn't you be both referring to notes and if necessary taking them?

Silence can also be useful in a stress interview. As we have already said most people do not like silences. Try it on a friend by suddenly pausing for a moment on the telephone. It's odds on that they will immediately break down into a stream of meaningless babble, the reason being that they feel uncomfortable – or perhaps they think the phone has been disconnected. Either way it should work. Now if you're in a pressure interview one of the things your interviewer will be trying to do is to see how you react. But if you can use silence to your advantage you could well turn the tables. In a more normal interview a pause will allow you time to think for a minute and if you find yourself forgetting what you were going to say next, you always have your notebook to refer to.

Appearance Counts

Appearance at an interview is very important. Some people claim that they know within one minute whether they are going to appoint a person or not (first impressions . . .). This might be something of an exaggeration but there is no point in ruining things by not taking the appropriate steps. You don't have to dress up in a £500 suit, an £80 shirt and a £100 pair of shoes; all you have to do is look clean, tidy and presentable.

Watch Your Vices

Don't let your vices get the better of you. You should not smoke unless the interviewer does. Nowadays it is increasingly uncommon for people to smoke and they certainly don't want their offices polluted by some precocious interviewee with absolutely no manners. After all, he might upset a client by acting in the same way.

Drinks are a different matter. Some people think you should decline because it destroys the momentum of the interview and those horrible slurping noises do not go down at all well. Really it's up to you. In the first place, if they offer you a cup it's odds on that the reason is that they want one! Second, drinks are excellent devices for creating a pause when you have completely forgotten what you were going to say next. They provide a good excuse for a silence!

The subject of alcohol is slightly more complicated. If you can't handle your booze, face up to it and stick to the soft drinks. Otherwise the chances are that you will make a complete idiot of yourself. Don't be fooled into drinking at lunch time if the interview was in the morning. You might let your guard down, but more importantly, some firms have a nasty habit of then revealing that you have a second interview in the afternoon — a daunting prospect if you've just drunk four pints of strong ale and your interviewer is stone cold sober! If you can handle your booze then you might as well go for it. In some companies and some professions an ability to handle your drink is a definite asset.

You should try to get rid of nervous habits during an interview. This is a problem area because the very fact that they are habits means that you may be unaware of them and they will be very difficult to eradicate altogether. An excellent tool to help you is the video recorder. If you have access to one, or your careers office has one, see if you can set up a dummy interview. This will usually be very embarrassing but, equally, very helpful in demonstrating your shortcomings in an interview situation. Nervous laughter is perhaps the most common of these problems. It is important to do your best to control this.

It's a Two-way Process

One thing you should always bear in mind vis-à-vis interviews is that they are a two-way process. You are interviewing them as much as they are interviewing you. This is obvious, and a lot of people accept it but do not apply it, simply because they are anxious to get a job and they don't really care where. Try to eliminate thoughts like this from your mind.

If you are not happy at the company you are working for then the chances of ever progressing are significantly diminished. It is absolutely imperative not only to find a job you enjoy but also people you enjoy working with. Of course, this is virtually impossible to assess on the strength of just two or three interviews but it is up to you to find out as much as possible. This should also help you because, by asking the interviewer questions, you can take control of the interview to some extent, which is important.

Furthermore, you can ask questions about the interviewer. It is perfectly acceptable to ask interviewers what they enjoy about their work, what they don't like, what their background is and so on. By doing this you will at the same time be playing on one of the great truths of human nature: people like talking about themselves. If you ask them a number of reasonably intelligent and searching questions they will be able to open up. As they do so they will warm to you because they have the opportunity to talk about themselves. If you don't think that quite fits then remember that finance is essentially a people business. It's important to get on with your fellow man and by chatting politely to your interviewer that's exactly what you will be doing. It's also very important because, as most people in the finance world know, the work itself is relatively easy. It might be a little trite to suggest that the more mystique a profession has the easier it is to do the job but there is something in it. At university you don't do special courses in stockbroking or Eurobond dealing. They are highly specialised disciplines which are learned on the job and, provided they have a modicum of intelligence most people can do them. In fact, in some instances, the ability or tendency to think before you act is a definite disadvantage! That being the case, prospective employers are going to look for the simple things in life, such as someone they like, can trust and can rely on to get on with the job when they have received sufficient training.

Make Yourself Look Wanted

A final tip which you might try in any interview is to make yourself look as much in demand as possible. They will usually ask you a question such as, 'Have you talked to any other companies in the same line of business?' Don't answer by saying, 'No. I applied to X, Y and Z but none of them has asked me for an interview'. Make it sound good.'I'm still waiting to hear from X, Y and Z' (this implies you have already had an interview and you are waiting to see whether they will take you on or not). If your conscience will allow you, why not lie? 'X rejected me but Y and Z have made me offers.' Even if you have had a terrible interview they have got to take you seriously because their rivals have obviously spotted something in you that they haven't .

Now this might all sound morally reprehensible but you have to remember that in the City there are some very fine distinctions between telling the 'truth'–whatever that may be–being 'economical' with the truth, and telling an out and out lie. When you get your job, in many instances you will find that it suits your purposes to look at these fine distinctions and completely ignore them. After all, if your boss asks you to get hold of a piece of information or else you can collect your P45 and the only way of getting it is to tell a 'subtle untruth', what course of action are you likely to take? This isn't to say that the City has no morals whatsoever; it *does* mean that where big money is involved people expect results and they are not necessarily too fussy about how they get them.

If You Are Rejected Find Out Why

Once the interview is over you have to wait and see what the final outcome is. If you don't hear after a couple of weeks, phone up to find out what happened. If you have not been accepted try to find out why. This could, of course, be embarrassing and difficult to do, but could be very useful if the people are frank and honest with you. Finding out the mistakes you made will help to stop you making them at your next interview.

There is probably no such thing as the perfect interview technique. However, you can improve your chances by following a few basic guidelines. If you don't succeed, don't look on it as a major defeat. If to you it is, then the chances are that you are approaching the whole exercise with the wrong attitude. It is not a 'test' of any description: it is an informal chat to see whether you and the employer can get together in a profitable relationship of mutual benefit. If they can't satisfy you then you should reject them just as surely as they will reject you if they don't think that you can work well with them.

Typical Questions Asked at Interviews

Why do you want to work here?

What makes you think you will make a good (securities analyst/ financial journalist etc?)

Where do you want to be in five years' time?

Why did you take these A levels/this degree?

What do you do in your spare time?

Tell me about yourself.

Do you think you'll have any trouble adjusting to life in London?

Are you decisive?

Are you familiar with word processors/personal computers?

What do you know about this firm?

Do you participate in any sports?

Why should we take you on at this firm?

Have you had any other job offers yet?

Which other firms have you applied to?

Have you had any other interviews yet? How did they go?

What did you get out of university?

What did you do in your holidays while you were at university?

Does travelling bother you?

What qualities has your degree subject given you which will make you a success in this field?

How competitive are you?

Questions to Ask at an Interview

What qualifications will you expect me to take?

How much time will I get to study for them?

Who pays for the training?

What happens if I fail?

How much of the training is on the job and how much is formal?

How long does it normally take before completion of training?

During training will I get exposure to a number of different parts of the organisation?

After training how much exposure will I get to other parts of the organisation?

How to Get a Highly Paid Job in the City

How long will it be after formal training is completed before I get 'real' responsibility?

How much attention do you pay to continuing professional training?

What is your drop-out rate after six months/one year/five years? Is this normal for your sort of business?

Why do people leave your firm?

Are your rates of pay competitive with other firms in the same line of business?

Who are your main competitors? Why do you think that you are a better employer than them?

Why should your clients choose you instead of another firm?

How much client contact will my work involve?

What size teams will I be working in?

Is there a great deal of travelling involved?

Is there opportunity to travel or work abroad within this firm/ profession?

What are the most important changes that are taking place within your industry at the present time?

Where do you see this industry being in five/ten years' time?

How well equipped is your firm to cope with these changes?

What sort of opportunities exist to change direction within the firm if I become dissatisfied with the nature of the work that I am doing?

What sort of opportunities exist outside this particular business for someone who has worked in it for a number of years and wishes to change direction?

How long does it take to reach director/partner level at your firm?

How did you get into this field?

Why did you get into this field?

Do you enjoy your job?

What is the single most exciting aspect of the job that you do?

What is the least attractive feature of your job?

If you were to have your time again, would you still work in the same line of business?

Useful Terms

Any profession or industry will have its own jargon and the world of finance is no exception. Before you set out on your job hunt you should try to familiarise yourself with as much of the jargon as possible. The following list explains some of the terms which you are most likely to come across.

Audit. It is a statutory requirement that every limited company in the UK has its financial records checked every year by qualified and independent specialists. This procedure is called the audit and is designed to ensure that the company's accounts give a 'true and fair' view of its financial position as at the company's year end.

Bear market. This occurs when the stock market is going down. A bear is a pessimist who believes that share prices are in a downward trend.

Big bang. For many years the City had enjoyed the benefits of archaic working practices which included the maintenance of minimum commission scales for stockbrokers on share purchases and sales. This meant that there was no possibility of effective competition between stockbrokers by lowering commissions. With the increase in international trading it was obvious that this state of affairs could not persist and the system was scrapped. This had a number of effects, the most important being that outsiders were allowed to buy stockbroking firms and the old rule that a firm could act as both a stockbroker (rather like a retailer of shares) and a stockjobber (rather like a wholesaler and only allowed to sell to stockbrokers) at the same time was rescinded.

Bull market. This occurs when the stockmarket is going up. A bull is an optimist who thinks that share prices are in an upward trend.

Equity. At the end of a financial year when a company has paid

123

all its outstanding obligations, the residual profit is available for distribution to the people who hold equity (shares) in the company in proportion to their holding. Similarly, if the company is being closed down then the residual assets after every debt has been met are available for distribution to people holding equity in the company. To all intents and purposes an equity and a share are one and the same thing.

Firm. Another word for a partnership. Firms differ from companies because in firms ownership and management are one and the same thing.

FT 30 Index. An index calculated hourly which measures the performance of the share prices of 30 leading UK industrial companies.

Gilt. A gilt is a security which is issued by the government when it wishes to borrow money. Gilts pay a fixed rate of interest and are traded on the stock market in the same way as shares. As a general rule, the price of a gilt will fluctuate according to the direction of interest rates. If interest rates go up the price of the gilt will go down, and vice versa.

Index linking. Typical examples here are gilt edged securities and Civil Service pensions. In the case of gild edged securities there is a special class of index-linked gilts whose value and the interest payment which it gives out are both linked to the Retail Price Index. That way the ravages of inflation can be mitigated.

Institution. A financial organisation which has a large amount of money to invest. Typical examples are pension funds and insurance companies. Nowadays these 'professional' investors dominate the UK stock market.

Investment trust. A company whose sole objective is to invest in the shares of other companies. As such they are very similar in nature to unit trusts.

LIFFE. The London International Financial Futures Exchange. In the 1970s as interest and exchange rates started to fluctuate quite violently there developed a need for major financial institutions and large companies to be able to secure either a exchange rate or a rate of interest in advance. LIFFE was formed with this in mind and is gradually becoming part of 'the global market' which makes it possible for trade to be carried out on a 24-hour basis.

Market maker. By making a market in a particular share or gilt a stockbroking company is in the position that it will either buy or sell shares from all comers.

PLC. A Public Limited Company is one whose shares can be offered to and bought by the public. All companies whose shares are traded on the Stock Exchange are by definition PLCs.

Portfolio. This refers to the total of the various investment holdings which a particular investor or institution holds. In some cases this will be further subdivided into, for example, portfolios of shares.

Privatisation. This is the process by which the government sells its holding in a nationalised or state controlled company to the public at large by selling the shares on the stock market.

Share. When a company is started up the money which investors put in to finance it, usually referred to as start-up capital, is divided into shares. A share will then define the interest which you have in a company. This interest includes the right to receive the dividends declared for the type of share that you hold and a right to vote at general meetings, unless you have non-voting shares.

Stock. In common parlance the terms stock and share are synonymous. In fact there is a slight difference in that the term stock is used when a security is denominated in units of £100. Usually, stocks are fixed interest securities.

Technical analysis. Technical analysts — or chartists — use graphs showing the historical price movements to try to determine future price movements. By looking at historical performance the analyst is watching buying and selling forces in the market and trying to establish a trend.

Underwriter. Investors–usually financial institutions such as merchant banks—who agree to purchase any shares or bonds offered for sale in a company which are not sold to the public. This ensures that whether or not the issue is a success the company which is raising the money will at least get the full amount. The underwriters are taking a calculated risk in such circumstances and will naturally charge the appropriate fee for their services.

Unit trust. This is a pooled investment vehicle similar to an investment trust. Investors who do not have the time or the expertise to manage their own savings can use a unit trust to provide a professional management service. Basically, investors buy units in the trusts and the money is then invested (usually in shares) by the fund managers.

The Unlisted Securities Market (USM). Until the USM was started in 1980 it was difficult for small companies to raise money by selling shares because they didn't have the track record or couldn't afford the expense of a full listing on the Stock Exchange. To get around this problem a rival to the Stock Exchange called the Over the Counter (OTC) market was formed. This worried the Stock Exchange for two reasons. First it was additional competition and second, the OTC market was not as well regulated as the Stock Exchange. So in 1983 the Stock Exchange created the USM. This has less stringent entry requirements and is cheaper than a full listing. At the same time it gives a company access to the capital markets.

The Kogan Page Career Series

This series consists of short guides (96-160 pages) to different careers for school-leavers, graduates and anyone wanting to start anew. Each book serves as an introduction to a particular career and to jobs available within that field, including full details of training qualifications and courses. The following 'Careers in' titles are available in paperback.

Accountancy *(2nd edition)*
Agriculture and Agricultural Sciences
Alternative Medicine
Antiques
Architecture
The Army
Art and Design *(4th edition)*
Aviation
Banking
Business
Catering and Hotel Management
  (2nd edition)
The Church
Civil Engineering
Civil Service
Classical Music
Computing and Information
  Technology
Conservation *(2nd edition)*
Crafts
Dance
Electrical and Electronic Engineering
  (2nd edition)
Engineering *(3rd edition)*
Eye Care
Fashion
Film Industry
Floristry and Retail Gardening
Hairdressing and Beauty
  Therapy *(3rd edition)*
Holiday Industry
Home Economics *(2nd edition)*
Journalism *(2nd edition)*
Land and Property
The Law *(2nd edition)*
Librarianship and Information
  Science *(2nd edition)*
Local Government *(2nd edition)*
Marketing, Public Relatins and
  Advertising *(2nd edition)*

Medicine, Dentistry and Mental
  Health *(3rd edition)*
Modelling
Museums and Art Galleries
Music Business
Nursing and Allied Professions
  (3rd edition)
Oil and Gas
Pharmacy
Photography *(2nd edition)*
The Police Force *(2nd edition)*
Politics
Printing
Psychology
Publishing
Retailing *(2nd edition)*
Road Transport
At Sea
Secretarial and Office Work
  (2nd edition)
Social Work *(2nd edition)*
Sport *(2nd edition)*
Surveying
Teaching *(2nd edition)*
Telecommunications
Television and Radio
The Theatre *(2nd edition)*
Using Biology
Using Languages *(2nd edition)*
Using Mathematics
Veterinary Surgery
Working Abroad
Working Outdoors *(3rd edition)*
Working with Animals *(3rd edition)*
Working with Children and Young
  People *(3rd edition)*
Working with the Disabled
Working with Horses

Also Available from Kogan Page